'A great read – pu
accessible for any
most influential r
Simon Guillebau

'This little book
Bible is not just one of the greatest books ever written,
head and shoulders above every other piece of literature,
with John's Gospel right at its heart, but the 'I am'
statements are right at the heart of John's Gospel. So . . .
how good and important is this book?'
Andy Hawthorne, CEO, The Message Trust

'What is Jesus all about and what does faith in him offer?
This would be the perfect book to give to someone who
wants to know more.'
Andrew Hill, Executive Director, Soldiers' and
Airmen's Scripture Readers Association

'Many people have all kinds of questions about the
meaning and purpose of life. My friend Marcus Nodder
tries, in this honest, concise, and readable book, to
answer those questions by looking at the claims of Jesus
Christ, about who he is and what he did two thousand
years ago. Even if you are sceptical as to the relevance of
Jesus to your life today, I invite you to have a go at
reading the book to see what you think. Decide for
yourself.'
Jeremy Marshall, businessman and evangelist

'As an evangelist, I am constantly on the lookout for good books to read and give away to not-yet-Christians. This is quite possibly the best I have ever come across.'
Mitch, evangelist, Crown Jesus Ministries

'By taking us to the words of Jesus, this outstanding and short book spells out the content and benefits of the Christian good news. It does so with compelling clarity. I will be buying several copies to give to friends – and encouraging those in our church to do the same.'
William Taylor, Rector, St Helen's, Bishopsgate, London

'Marcus Nodder has a wonderfully compelling formula: some pictures with which we've all been familiar since childhood – lights, doors and shepherds. He shows how Jesus used them to point to himself, and then Marcus reveals, with a staggering array of stimulating illustrations, why that is exactly what we need in terms of our longings for things such as meaning, freedom, truth, and hope in an increasingly bewildering world.'
Rico Tice, Senior Minister for Evangelism, All Souls, Langham Place, London, and co-author of *Christianity Explored*

'I strongly recommend you read this book if you are not a Christian; by doing so, you will read some of the claims and promises that Jesus made about himself. Only Jesus can give satisfying answers to the meaning and purpose of life.'
Jane Tooher, Director, Priscilla and Aquila Centre, Diocese of Sydney, Australia

I AM.

The answer to life's biggest questions

Marcus Nodder

INTER-VARSITY PRESS
36 Causton Street, London SW1P 4ST, England
Email: ivp@ivpbooks.com
Website: www.ivpbooks.com

The author and publisher have made every effort to ensure that the external
website addresses included in this book are correct and up to date at the time
of going to press. The author and publisher are not responsible for the content,
quality or continuing accessibility of the sites.

Unless otherwise indicated, Scripture quotations are from The Holy Bible,
English Standard Version, copyright © 2001 by Crossway, a publishing
ministry of Good News Publishers. Used by permission. All rights reserved.
Emphasis added by Marcus Nodder.

Extracts marked KJV are from the Authorized Version of the Bible (The King
James Bible), the rights in which are vested in the Crown, and are reproduced
by permission of the Crown's Patentee, Cambridge University Press.

The extract from the Committal in the service for the Burial of the Dead
in *An English Prayer Book* is copyright © Church Society 1994.

Every effort has been made to seek permission to use copyright material
reproduced in this book. The publisher apologizes for those cases where
permission might not have been sought and, if notified, will formally
seek permission at the earliest opportunity.

First published in 2021

British Library Cataloguing-in-Publication Data
A catalogue record for this book is available from the British Library.

ISBN: 978–1–78974–177–3
eBook ISBN: 978–1–78974–178–0

Set in Minion Pro 10.25/13.5 pt
Typeset in Great Britain by CRB Associates, Potterhanworth, Lincolnshire
Printed in Great Britain by Ashford Colour Press Ltd, Gosport, Hampshire

Produced on paper from sustainable forests.

*Inter-Varsity Press publishes Christian books that are true to the Bible
and that communicate the gospel, develop discipleship and strengthen
the church for its mission in the world.*

*IVP originated within the Inter-Varsity Fellowship, now the Universities and
Colleges Christian Fellowship, a student movement connecting Christian
Unions in universities and colleges throughout Great Britain, and a member
movement of the International Fellowship of Evangelical Students. Website:
www.uccf.org.uk. That historic association is maintained, and all senior
IVP staff and committee members subscribe to the UCCF Basis of Faith.*

'Truly, truly, I say to you,
before Abraham was, I am.'

Jesus

| CONTENTS

INTRODUCTION

'I'm really sorry, but I don't take marketing calls, so I'm going to hang up now.'

It's my standard response to the 'Hello, am I speaking to Mr Noodle/Noddler/Nibbler/Nodder?' telemarketing line. I'm not rude, but I'm also not into wasting time – theirs or mine. I'm pretty sure that whatever they're selling is something I neither need nor want. So, not interested.

Some think that way about God, that he's just after things from you – your time, your money, your life – things you'd rather keep, thank you very much. And you think that whatever he happens to be offering is not anything you're going to need or want any time soon. So, you hang up – or don't bother to pick up in the first place. Nowadays, it's more likely to be a case of apathe-ism than atheism.

But could it be that what's on offer is different from what many imagine?

The focus of the Bible is a unique intervention of God in human history in the person of Jesus Christ. The whole point of it was not to take from us, but to give to us; to give us things we really need, things we long for.

At the heart of the teaching of Jesus, recorded in the Bible in John's Gospel, are eight statements beginning with the words 'I am'. In each of them, Jesus reveals who he is and what he can do for us. He claims to be able to meet our deepest needs and desires as human beings – for meaning, purpose, hope, forgiveness, truth, life, to name but a few. This isn't just another marketing call.

The Times newspaper once wrote to eminent writers and thinkers asking them what was wrong with the world. Apparently, the author G. K. Chesterton wrote back with the simple, and humble, reply: 'I am.' But if, instead, the question had asked what the solution was to humanity's problems, who would have dared to reply, 'I am'? And who would have been taken seriously if he or she had? Yet that is what Jesus outrageously claimed.

King Tarquin was one of the kings of Ancient Rome. The legend goes that, one day, an old woman came to him in his palace, carrying nine books. She offered them to him, but the price she demanded was so high that he laughed in her face. Without a word, the old woman burned three of the books to ashes before his eyes. She then offered him the remaining volumes, still at the same price as before. This time the king laughed even more, thinking her crazy. At once, she burned another three and calmly repeated her request.

Tarquin now became more serious and thoughtful, nervous of what he might be turning down. So he bought the remaining three books at the price that had been asked for all nine. Taking the money, the old woman vanished, never to be seen again. The writings turned out to be none other than the Sibylline Books, priceless prophecies about the future of Rome.[1]

Just as Tarquin laughed at the old woman, so also many people don't have much time for Jesus. They assume that what he's offering is of little value but perhaps, like the king, without really knowing what it is they're turning down. In the end, Tarquin's curiosity got the better of him, and he was staggered by what he found. It was so very different from what he had imagined. Countless people have made the same discovery with Jesus – the Jesus of history.

A life of seventy years lasts just over 600,000 hours. Spending a few of them taking a closer look at what Jesus offers is surely worth the investment. And that is what this book is about.

I am THE BREAD

John 6:35

> My question – that which at the age of fifty brought me to the verge of suicide – was the simplest of questions, lying in the soul of every man ... 'Is there any meaning in my life that the inevitable death awaiting me does not destroy?'[1]

So wrote the great Russian novelist Leo Tolstoy in his book *A Confession*. By middle age, he had achieved all the goals he had set himself as an ambitious young man: a successful career, with fame as a writer, thanks to his doorstop of a novel *War and Peace*; he was respected and wealthy; he had a happy family, with a wife and fourteen children; and he was as fit as a fiddle, physically and mentally. He'd done it all – had it all. And, suddenly, it hit him – a hunger; an emptiness.

He quoted an Eastern fable to picture our condition. He said that it's as if you're in a dry well, hanging from a flimsy branch in the wall. At the bottom, underneath you, is a dragon, ready to swallow you. And two mice – one white, one black – are circling round the stem of your branch gnawing away at it. Soon, it's going to snap off and you're going to fall into the dragon's jaws. But then, as you hang there, you notice some honey on the leaves of the branch and you start licking it. He said:

> So I too clung to the twig of life, knowing that the dragon of death was inevitably awaiting me, ready to tear me to pieces ... I tried to lick the honey which formerly consoled me, but the honey no longer gave me pleasure, and the white and black mice of day and night gnawed at the branch by which I hung. I saw the dragon clearly and the honey no longer tasted sweet. I only saw the unescapable dragon and the mice, and I could not tear my gaze from them ...
>
> The two drops of honey which had diverted my eyes from the cruel truth longer than the rest: my love of family, and of writing ... were no longer sweet to me.[2]

Few of us are great Russian novelists, but many of us will be able to relate to Tolstoy's experience of spiritual hunger. Some become aware of it when they, like him, have achieved many of their goals and suddenly think, 'What was the point? Why am I not satisfied?'

Some time ago, I watched an interview with Tom Brady, the US National Football League (NFL) player and one of the USA's biggest sports stars. At the time, he had three Superbowl wins to his name, had made more money than he could have ever dreamed of, and was dating a Brazilian supermodel. Everyone wanted to be around him. He was considered the most eligible bachelor in the country. With all his money, fame, and career accomplishments, Tom acknowledged that many would assume he was living the dream. But he commented, 'Me, I think, God, it's gotta be more than this.'

'What's the answer?' asked the interviewer.

'I wish I knew. I wish I knew,' Tom replied, with a tone of desperation and longing.

For others, who haven't reached the top, it's more of a shadow in the soul in the day-to-day. You work, you eat, you play, you sleep, and then get up and do it again. And again. And again. You do your best to be happy, but you can't help but think, 'What's all this for? Isn't there more to life than this?'

Hunger is one of our most basic cravings, and one of the first we experience. Think of babies: they experience hunger; they want food; they cry until they get it. But there is another type of hunger that we become aware of as we grow up – a spiritual hunger; a hunger not in our stomach but in our soul. A hunger for meaning, for purpose; a longing for more; a feeling of being empty within, even when our bellies are full. How can we satisfy this spiritual hunger?

Soul food

Jesus said, 'I am the bread of life; whoever comes to me shall not hunger, and whoever believes in me shall never thirst' (John 6:35). Jesus claimed that he is the food we need. As we come to him and put our trust in him, we find the satisfaction for our deepest spiritual longings. He fills the emptiness within. He gives us inner peace. In him, we find the answer to the big questions of life.

People who go on safari in Africa search for the 'big five' – the lion, leopard, rhino, elephant, and buffalo. But the ultimate safari is looking for answers to the big five questions of life: the question of origins ('Where have I come from?'); of destiny ('Where am I going?'); of identity ('Who am I?'); of meaning ('What is the purpose of life?'); and of ethics ('How should I live?'). Not having satisfying answers to these big questions leaves us spiritually hungry. Jesus said that he is the answer to all of them: 'I am the bread of life; whoever comes to me shall not hunger.' It's a wonderful promise.

Jonathan Aitken was a high-flying UK politician, a member of the Cabinet, tipped to be the next Prime Minister. He wrote:

> The more my career prospered on the surface, the more my deeper feelings were signalling an empti-ness and lack of fulfilment within ... Gnawing away at me inside was a problem I could not describe, except by giving it psychobabble labels such as 'lack of inner peace', 'emptiness of feeling', 'hollowness of spirit', or more simply 'something missing'. It was as though, after spending a life-time wanting to climb a particular mountain, I had unexpectedly reached the final approach to its

summit, only to discover that there was nothing there worth the effort of the ascent.[3]

It was by putting his trust in Jesus that he came to experience an inner peace he had never known before. Jesus gives us this peace, and satisfies our inner hunger and thirst, through the gift of the Holy Spirit to live in us and fill us: 'If anyone thirsts, let him come to me and drink. Whoever believes in me . . . "Out of his heart will flow rivers of living water." Now this he said about the Spirit' (John 7:37–39).

Dragon slayer

As the bread of life, Jesus not only satisfies our spiritual hunger, he also gives us eternal life. He deals with the death problem, which we all face, whether or not we feel the inner emptiness. Jesus says:

> The bread of God is he who comes down from heaven and *gives life to the world* . . . I am the living bread that came down from heaven. If anyone eats of this bread, *he will live for ever*.
> (John 6:33, 51)

The solution to our problem has to deal not just with the inner hunger but also with death – the dragon at the bottom of the well – because it's death that makes every-thing so meaningless, if that is the end. As the bread of life, Jesus says that he can give us eternal life.

So, bread is not just a picture of satisfying hunger. Bread represents the food you need to stay alive. Bread is a staple food. Jesus didn't say, 'I am the vanilla slice', 'I am the jam doughnut', or 'I am the chocolate éclair' – a naughty-but-nice treat. He's the bread of life. Without him we're dead – spiritually, eternally. For centuries in Europe, bread was the main source of food for poor peasants and the working classes. Bread was a big deal. It was a life-and-death issue. That's the picture spiritually. Jesus is the bread of life.

We're hanging from the twig. The dragon of death is underneath. Through his death and resurrection, Jesus slays the dragon, gives us eternal life, and rescues us from eternal death.

Sole supplier

He's the only one who can. Jesus says, 'I am *the* bread of life'. He's not just the *bread* of life. He's *the* bread of life – the one and only. *The* bread that we need. Standing in the bread aisle in the supermarket can be a daunting experience. So many options. White or brown? Thick or thin sliced? This brand or that one? Wholemeal or rye? Free-range bread that's spent a happy life walking around in a field or . . . It's not like that spiritually. Jesus says he is the one and only bread of life. It's an exclusive claim. What he offers cannot be obtained anywhere else. But why is that?

Part of the answer is found in his unique origin. He alone has come down from heaven. He alone is God come to earth. He says, 'The bread of God is he who comes down from heaven' (John 6:33). For someone to be the bread of life, he or she has to have come from heaven because only God himself can satisfy our spiritual hunger. Only the author of life can give us eternal life. The whole reason we are spiritually hungry and die is because our relationship with God has been broken. We were made by God for God. So the solution is the restoring of that relationship, through God becoming man in Jesus, coming to rescue us; through this death and resurrection.

Tolstoy said, 'All that time . . . my heart was oppressed with a painful feeling, which I can only describe as a search for God.'[4] By coming to Jesus, our search reaches its destination. He is the bread of life come down from heaven. Or so he claimed.

How do we know he's telling the truth? He could have been deluded – or lying. Anyone can claim to be the bread of life. Where's the proof?

Just before Jesus made his claim, he fed five thousand people with five loaves and two fish; the people ate until they were full. Twelve baskets of leftovers were picked up at the end of the meal. It was a miracle. It was proof that Jesus is the bread of life. The physical demonstration proved he could do the spiritual reality.

If you go for a job interview, you need to give proof of your skills and abilities. It cuts no ice at all just to say, 'I'm a great team player.' Any recruiters worth their salt will say, 'Give us an example. Give us evidence of that.' So you tell them, 'Well, there was this situation at work and this is how I handled it. And here's a reference from my boss.'

Jesus doesn't just say, 'I'm bread of life.' He demonstrates it. He gives us evidence so that we might believe. The feeding miracle is the proof to back up the claim, as are all his miracles. They are worth a closer look by reading through John's Gospel.

Dinner time

If Jesus really is the bread of life, how should we respond? Jesus says, 'I am the bread of life; whoever *comes to me* shall not hunger, and whoever *believes in me* shall never thirst' (John 6:35). It's really very simple. We just need to come to Jesus; to believe in him. There aren't a hundred and one things we need to do. He doesn't say we need first to go away and clean up our act, sort our lives out, become more moral, or get religion. There's just one thing we need to do: come to him or believe in him – it's the same thing. It's very simple but life-changing.

Believing, though, is more than ticking a mental box. It means having a personal trust in him. Jesus says, 'I am the living bread that came down from heaven. If anyone *eats of this bread*, he will live for ever' (John 6:51). Feeding on the bread is a picture of receiving Jesus personally, not just saying, 'Yes, I believe he existed' or even just 'I believe it is true that he is the bread of life'. More than that, it is personally trusting in him – receiving him.

Sometimes, children are hungry at the end of a meal because they've sat there with the food in front of them but haven't eaten it. They've acknowledged the existence of the food but have just pushed it around the plate. So, acknowledging Jesus existed, or even that he is the bread of life, is not enough. We need to feed, receive, trust personally that Jesus is for each of us. He came for me.

And this believing in him is believing that he came to die for me. That's why he switches from talking about bread to talking about his body. He says, 'Whoever feeds on my flesh and drinks my blood has eternal life' (John 6:54). It may sound like cannibalism but it's just a picture. He's speaking of his death on the cross. We're each to believe personally in that – that he died for me and my wrongdoing; to pay for it, to rescue me from the judgment I deserve. Communion (when Christians eat bread and wine at church) pictures this personal trust in, and feeding on, Christ and his death for us.

Some friends kindly took me and some others out for a meal in a fine restaurant. We ate – they paid. It's a beautiful arrangement! And so it is with Jesus: we eat – he pays; he picks up the tab. Through his death we have life. What's not to like? But not everyone does like it. And not everyone did at the time. Why was that?

Perishable food

Jesus said to the crowd following him:

> You are seeking me, not because you saw signs, but because you ate your fill of the loaves. Do not

labour for the food that perishes, but for the food
that endures to eternal life, which the Son of Man
will give to you.
(John 6:26–27)

Many had no time for Jesus as the bread of life. They
just wanted free food. They'd been at the feeding of the
five thousand and thought, 'This is awesome. Free
meals.' All they were thinking of was their bellies – the
material, not the spiritual. It's easy to make the same
mistake today – to think that material things can satisfy
our deepest needs.

I asked Siri on my phone what the meaning of life
was. She said, 'All evidence to date suggests it's chocolate.' Obviously, it was just a joke but there's a serious
side to it. Can material things give my life meaning
and answer the big questions? Adverts imply that they
can. They show us pictures of people who are happy
because they have a new thing. The message is that
if only you get this new shampoo, or coffee, or car,
or house, or lottery win, then you'll be happy. But it's a
lie. Material things cannot satisfy our deepest needs.
It's licking the honey when you're hanging from the
twig.

Sometimes, people even try to reinvent Jesus to con-
form to this agenda. It's as if he's come just to improve
our lot in life materially – to give us health, wealth, and
happiness, rather than eternal life. But that's just making
up your own religion.

Hard to swallow

There's another reason, too, why people reject Jesus. 'After this many of his disciples turned back and no longer walked with him' (John 6:66). Why? Because they found some of the things Jesus taught hard. 'When many of his disciples heard it, they said, "This is a hard saying; who can listen to it?"' (6:60). It was hard to understand and hard to accept. They grumbled about his claim to have come from heaven (6:41). They 'disputed among themselves saying "How can this man give us his flesh to eat?"' (6:52). Jesus asked, 'Do you take offence at this?' (6:61). Many did, and many still do today. They're offended by what Jesus taught.

The Bible has some hard things to say about God – that he is holy and pure, and judges and rules; about us – that we are not the good people we like to think we are, but have rebelled against God and deserve judgment; about eternity – that there is heaven and hell; about Jesus – that he is the only way to God; about lifestyle – that there is right and wrong, and that God can tell us what we do with our money, our time, our relationships, and our sexuality. Many take offence and turn away. But the question is not whether it is comfortable but whether it is true.

The doctor told me that I had high cholesterol and needed to cut back on the cheese. It was a hard saying; it was very inconvenient and not what I wanted to hear. I love cheese. I used to eat it morning, noon, and night.

But to ignore the truth can be fatal. The same principle applies spiritually.

Sadly, Tolstoy did ignore the truth. Although he had his spiritual crisis and turned to God, he didn't like a lot of what he found in the Gospels – the hard sayings. So what did he do? He rewrote it. He produced his own version – Tolstoy's Gospel: *The Gospel in Brief*, it's called. He took out all the bits he didn't like – as some people do today. But to do so is to reject the real Jesus.

What should we do then? At the end of chapter 6 of John's Gospel, Jesus turns to his twelve closest followers. 'Do you want to go away as well?' he asks (John 6:67). Simon Peter answers him, 'Lord, to whom shall we go? You have the words of eternal life' (6:68).

That's the bottom line. If we reject Jesus, what's the alternative? Whom are we going to follow instead? What do they offer? Can they deliver? Can they satisfy our deepest longings? Can they give us eternal life?

Jesus said, 'I am the bread of life; whoever comes to me shall not hunger, and whoever believes in me shall never thirst.'

I am THE LIGHT
John 8:12

One Christmas I joined a group who went carol singing to people who were housebound. It was a cold, dark winter's evening. One visit I will never forget was to an elderly widow. We filed into the living room where she was sitting in the dark. She was blind, so didn't have the lights on. A double darkness – in the dark, because blind, and sitting in the dark, too. A few carols later, we said our goodbyes, shuffled back out, and returned to the warmth of our brightly lit homes and families.

But for days, I couldn't get the image out of my mind of this blind woman sitting alone in the dark. What could be worse? But there *is* something worse. Far worse. Spiritual blindness; being in the dark spiritually.

Sometimes, people talk about 'feeling like mushrooms' in the workplace. You're kept in the dark and, once in a while, you have some manure thrown over you. I don't know whether that's an accurate description of mushroom cultivation, but it does seem to be a common enough experience at work. People refer to 'mushroom management', when managers don't tell you what's going on. You're given work without knowing what the purpose of it is. You're kept in the dark.

But feeling like a mushroom is not just a problem at work. It's a problem in life. Have you ever felt as if you're being kept in the dark, and that the management aren't really telling you what's going on in life? We get on with it – we eat, we work, we sleep, we go on holiday, we retire, and we die. But what's the big picture? What's the meaning of it all? What's the point? We're in the dark, and some manure is thrown over us from time to time, when things go wrong in life.

If you feel like a mushroom at work, you can go to speak to your manager or HR about it, or get a new job. But where do you go if you feel like a mushroom in life?

Jesus said, 'I am the light of the world. Whoever follows me will not walk in darkness, but will have the light of life' (John 8:12). Are you in the dark? Jesus is the light. But what exactly does he mean? And what if I don't feel like a mushroom? What if I don't feel in the dark? Of what relevance is he to me then?

Born blind

When Jesus made this claim about himself, 'he saw a man blind from birth' (John 9:1), who was sitting by the side of the road, begging. It isn't something you see very often in modern Western societies but, in less developed countries, a blind beggar at the roadside is sadly all too common. How awful such a life must be. Imagine yourself in that situation: a life lived in the dark, totally dependent on others; blind from birth, unable to see your friends or spouse or children; unable to see the beauty of a flower or a sunset, or the stars at night.

It's very sad and very relevant because blindness is actually a picture of the human condition. According to the World Health Organization, 36 million people in the world are registered blind. But according to the Bible, the 7.8 billion people alive today were born blind. Everyone is blind from birth – not physically, but spiritually. This blind beggar whom Jesus met by the roadside, sitting in the dark, was physically blind, and we may pity him. But the Bible effectively says to everyone, 'That's you, that is. That's your spiritual state. Blind from birth and in the dark.'

Darkness is a theme that runs through John's Gospel. The book begins by describing the world as a dark place. It says, 'The light [that is, Jesus] shines *in the darkness*, and the darkness has not overcome it' (John 1:5). It's speaking about a spiritual and moral darkness. Although we were made by God for God, we've gone our own way. We've rebelled against his loving rule. Because of this, the world has been plunged into spiritual darkness. God is light. Having rejected him, we find ourselves alienated from him and in the dark spiritually.

What this feels like on the ground, in experience, varies. Some people become aware of the darkness when they realize they don't have answers to the big questions. One man, who runs his own company, said this: 'I was in the gym on the treadmill, and I suddenly realized that I'm 49, on the treadmill of life, and haven't a clue where I'm going. I need answers. There's probably some good stuff in the Bible, so it's time I looked at it.'[1]

Another, a company chairman, explained, 'I was on my knees gardening at the weekend. It suddenly struck me that I've lost two friends to cancer, one friend to a heart attack, and another to a brain aneurism in the past year. I'm 62 and haven't a clue what I believe.' It was the beginning of his reading the Bible with a Christian friend.[2]

Lost in the dark

Jesus describes the experience of being in the dark in two ways. First, he says, 'If anyone walks in the night, he stumbles' (John 11:10). If it's dark and you can't see where you're going, you stumble and bump into things. I've lost count of the number of times I've whacked my shin on the corner of the bed, when getting up in the night without turning the light on. Perhaps you've had the experience of walking along a dark path at night in a forest. It's very easy to lose your footing and twist an ankle or fall flat on your face. It's very hard to walk properly and safely.

We're spiritually in the dark and so we stumble. We don't think and live as we should. We don't live to please God but ourselves. We don't love him and other people as we were created to. Our hearts and lives are darkened. We are spiritually blind.

Another way Jesus describes being in the dark is similar to this: 'The one who walks in the darkness does not know where he is going' (John 12:35). Has that ever happened to you? Have you ever got lost in the dark and confused or disorientated? Life apart from God is like that. We don't know where we're going. There is no ultimate direction, no map, and no signs. We're just wandering through life.

At a London Underground station, I once saw a blind man standing at an intersection of corridors at rush hour. There were crowds of people rushing here, there, and everywhere. There was so much noise and hustle and bustle, and this poor man was standing there, turning this way, then that. He was completely disorientated; lost; vulnerable. Thankfully someone went and took him by the arm to lead him out. But being spiritually blind is like that. We don't know where we're going in life. Sure, we may set ourselves goals – to be happy, to achieve this or that – but when it comes to ultimate direction, we're in the dark.

That's how Jesus describes the human condition apart from God. We're in the dark, spiritually blind from birth because of our rejection of God. We're in the dark in our thinking and our living.

But this present darkness is not our biggest problem. Jesus warned about a future, eternal darkness. It's something he referred to as 'the outer darkness', where there will be 'weeping and gnashing of teeth' (Matthew 8:12; 25:30): a place of ultimate alienation from God; a place of final separation from the light of his goodness; a place he called hell. That is what we are stumbling towards, like blind people walking towards a cliff edge.

In the first chapter, we were thinking about the 'hard sayings' of Jesus. Well, this is definitely one of them – what he teaches about eternity. God is just. Judgment is coming, regardless of how well we may think our lives are going at the moment. This is the problem that lies ahead – ultimate darkness after the present darkness. What is the solution?

Light of life

Jesus said, 'I am the light of the world. Whoever follows me will not walk in darkness, but will have the light of life' (John 8:12). Jesus has come to rescue us, from both the present and ultimate darkness. He is the light of world. If we follow him, we will enjoy the light of life, both now and eternally.

When Jesus hung on the cross, in the middle of the day darkness suddenly covered the land for three hours. Jesus, the light of the world, was dying in our place. He was experiencing the darkness caused by our wrongdoing, by our sin. He absorbed that darkness into himself. He paid the penalty that we deserve and was then raised to life, bursting out of the dark tomb of death. As the risen Lord, he is the light of the world.

If we follow him, we enjoy the light of life. We no longer stumble in the dark, but walk tall in the light – forgiven by God, knowing God as his children; knowing how to live in a way that pleases God, and changed by God to do that; knowing where we're going, with a clear sense of direction. We live for God, serve God, and are heading for eternity with him in the kingdom where he is light.

That's what Jesus as the light of the world can do for us – or so he claimed. How do we know he can deliver? Because of what happened to the blind man. Jesus said, 'As long as I am in the world, I am the light of the world' (John 9:5); he then made some mud, put it on the blind man's eyes, and told him to go and wash. 'So he went and washed and came back seeing' (9:7).

Jesus healed him. He opened his blind eyes. And what he did *physically* for that man, he can do *spiritually* for any of us. That's the point of the miracle. It's evidence – it's proof – that he really is the light of the world.

Switching on

The change from darkness to light which that man experienced physically, countless people have experienced since spiritually. Light has flooded into the darkness of their lives.

The book *Devil at My Heels* tells the life story of Louis Zamperini. During the Second World War, the plane he served on crashed into the Pacific. He survived forty-seven days adrift in a lifeboat, and then he endured two brutal years in a Japanese prisoner-of-war camp. He returned home a hero. But his hatred for one of his former captors took hold of him; his life spiralled downwards, with drunkenness and reckless behaviour. He came to believe that his only hope lay in murder. He was in deep darkness.

Then, suddenly, his life was transformed, and the darkness was flooded with light. Joy replaced anger in his heart. He freely forgave his former captors and a new life began. His marriage was saved and he was a faithful husband. He died in 2014 at the age of 97.

What brought about such a change?

In 1949, the US evangelist Billy Graham came to Los Angeles. Very reluctantly, Louis went along and heard about Jesus. This is his account of what happened:

> I dropped to my knees and for the first time in my life truly humbled myself before the Lord. I asked him to forgive me . . . for my sinful life. I made no excuses . . . He had said, 'Whosoever shall call upon the name of the Lord shall be saved,' so I took him at his word, begged for his pardon, and asked Jesus to come into my life.[3]

Following Jesus brought him out of the darkness into the light.

Follow me

The response Jesus calls for is simple but life-changing, as Louis Zamperini discovered. 'I am the light of the world. Whoever *follows me* will not walk in darkness' (John 8:12). He didn't mean follow him on Twitter or Facebook, but believe in him, trust in him, and live for him. Jesus said, 'I have come into the world as a light, so that whoever *believes in me* may not remain in darkness' (John 12:46). What a wonderful promise.

What's not to like? But many at the time didn't like it.

The London Project to Cure Blindness is a collaboration between two professors who believe that they can develop a cure for the largest cause of blindness in the developed world. If they can deliver, these two men are going to be heroes. But the response to Jesus healing a man blind from birth was vicious; it was not a celebration but a confrontation. It was greeted with outright hostility from the religious leaders, the Pharisees. They repeatedly interrogated the beggar Jesus had healed. They wouldn't accept his account of what had happened. They questioned his parents but still they wouldn't believe. And they ended up throwing the man out of the synagogue and plotting to kill Jesus. What was going on? Why did such a good deed by Jesus provoke such hostility?

A young man came to our church, did a course to find out more about Jesus, and started following him. When he told his non-Christian friends and colleagues that he was going to church and had decided to get baptized, he was taken aback by the strength of their reaction. 'You're out of your mind. You need to drink more,' his former drinking buddies scoffed.

Why such hostility to Jesus, both then and today?

Strange love

Jesus tells us: 'The light has come into the world, and people loved the darkness rather than the light because their works were evil. For everyone who does wicked things hates the light and does not come to the light, lest his works should be exposed' (John 3:19–20). We know God is there and we should be living for him, not for ourselves. We know we're doing wrong. We know we're not living as we should.

Like kids hiding in the dark when they've done something naughty, we don't want to be found out and exposed, so we run away from the light. Like burglars staying in the shadows, we try to hide from the search-light of the police helicopter overhead. The light is threatening to a world on the run from God. We hate the light. We love the dark.

Have you had that experience of thinking your windows at home are clean and then, on a bright sunny day, you suddenly see how dirty they are? We may think of ourselves as morally decent, upright people until the light of Jesus is switched on and exposes the dirt in our lives: our failure to love God and other people as we should; the selfishness, pride, envy, lust, and anger in our hearts.

But however uncomfortable that exposure may be, it's for our good. The light that exposes is the light that brings cleansing, healing, and life. If we reject this light, we stay in the dark – both now and eternally. If we reject Jesus, he becomes like a super-bright light that actually blinds us, as if looking at the sun through a telescope, which is not a clever thing to do – neither with the sun nor with the Son of God.

Jesus warns, 'For judgement I came into this world, that those who do not see may see, *and those who see may become blind*' (John 9:39). The religious leaders were such people. They were those 'who see' – that is to say, who thought they could see. They wouldn't accept they had a problem and that they were spiritually blind. They took offence at Jesus. They protested, outraged, 'Are we also blind?' (9:40). So, in judgment, they were plunged into even greater darkness. They became even blinder – blinded by the light. Jesus said to them, 'If you were blind, you would have no guilt; but now that you say, "We see", your guilt remains' (9:41).

Many people today are like those Pharisees back then. They reject the diagnosis. They take offence at Jesus. They won't accept that they are spiritually blind and in the dark. They think that they can see and are already enlightened.

The eighteenth-century movement in Europe, championing reason as the solution to everything, was known as the Enlightenment. The attitudes promoted at that time live on today: 'I'm intelligent and educated. I can work things out for myself and find my own solutions. Humanity can sort itself out unaided.' Alternatively, people claim to have found enlightenment through other philosophies, meditation, Eastern mysticism, and looking within.

But Jesus is saying that if we reject him, we are condemning ourselves to staying in the dark – now and for eternity. That's not what he wants, but the choice he puts before us is very stark. It's black and white; it's darkness and light. He urges us, even today, to choose wisely: 'I am the light of the world. Whoever follows me will not walk in darkness, but will have the light of life.'

I am THE DOOR
John 10:9

> Some prisoners will spend as many as 23 hours a
> day inside their two-person cell. With a bunk bed
> and toilet wedged into a 4m by 3m cell, the rela-
> tionship with your cellmate can turn a tough
> experience into a nightmare.[1]

This glimpse of prison life from Mark Lloyd, a former
soldier, who spent twenty weeks behind bars for fraud,
should make us glad that it's something most of us will
never have to go through.

Can you imagine how terrible it would be to lose
your freedom, to be locked up in a cell for most of the
day? You wouldn't be able to just go where you want,
when you want. You wouldn't be free to go for a walk
in the park on a sunny day. You would be forced to
endure whatever daytime television your cellmate
wanted to watch. 'What most do not understand', said
the mother of another prisoner, one serving a long
sentence, 'is that the lack of freedom is, in itself, a
huge punishment.' All of us have a hard-wired desire
for freedom, and having that freedom taken away is
unthinkable.

But that, some people claim, is precisely what Christianity does: it takes away your freedom. It imprisons people – not physically, but in the sense that it dictates what you must believe and how you must behave. Rules about belief and behaviour are seen by many as walls and bars that hem you in and restrict you. People don't want that. They want to be free to decide for themselves what is right and wrong, to live as they see fit. They don't want to operate according to what an ancient book says.

Now, the desire for freedom is good and natural. No-one wants to live behind bars. But the question is this: where is true freedom to be found? Is it in a life of doing whatever you want, or is it actually in a life of submitting to God and his authority?

Jesus said, 'I am the door. If anyone enters by me, he will be saved and will go in and out and find pasture . . . I came that they may have life and have it abundantly' (John 10:9–10). What Jesus promises is life – an abundant life of going in and out and finding pasture. That doesn't sound like prison at all; it sounds like freedom. So we would do well to take a closer look at what Jesus offers and to consider whether someone has actually switched the labels on the goods.

This 'I am' saying of Jesus comes in a chapter where he's using the picture of shepherds and sheep. When he says that he is the door (or gate), what he has in mind is the door of a sheepfold: 'I am the door of the sheep' (10:7). But what does he mean? How does it relate to this question of freedom?

28

Safe room

'I am the door. If anyone enters by me, he will be saved' (John 10:9). In this picture, we are sheep and Jesus is the door through whom we enter into the safety and protection of the sheepfold. But what is it that we are kept safe from in there?

First, we are protected from the thief who comes 'only to steal and kill and destroy' (10:10). This pictures those who, through false teaching, destroy people. The immediate reference is the religious leaders who led people astray. We'll consider some other examples in the next chapter, called 'I am the good shepherd'.

Second, we're saved from the wolf (10:12) who comes to snatch the sheep and scatter the flock. The wolf may be an image of the devil – elsewhere in the Bible he's described as a roaring lion, seeking someone to devour. Alternatively, the wolf may represent the eternal judgment to which we are heading because of our rejection of God. According to Jesus, that is the ultimate danger we face and from which we need saving. Salvation is contrasted with condemnation. Jesus said, 'God did not send his Son into the world to condemn the world, but in order that the world might be saved through him' (John 3:17). And, just after warning about judgment in the life to come, Jesus said, 'I say these things so that you may be saved' (John 5:34). Jesus is the door through whom we enter this place of safety, both now and eternally.

One Easter Sunday, a tornado ripped through a town in Mississippi, killing thirty-four people. A family of four sought refuge in a concrete safe room inside their home. Their house was destroyed in twenty seconds by the twister, but they survived the storm and emerged without a scratch. When the storm of the final judgment comes, we need to be in the spiritual safe room. Jesus is the door into it. If we enter through him, we will emerge without a scratch. But seeking refuge anywhere else is like taking shelter from a tornado in a tent or a portable loo.

To think of it another way – in the end, Jesus is the door into heaven itself, the ultimate place of safety. People speak about the pearly gates of heaven. Well, Jesus is the pearly gate. He's the way in.

So is Christianity restrictive? Well, is a sheepfold restrictive for sheep? Yes, but in a good way. If the sheep just roam free outside the sheep-pen at night, that's not freedom – it's suicide. That kind of freedom leaves nothing but a few bones and bits of wool by morning. So, spiritually, salvation, protection, safety, is found inside the sheepfold. Inside is life. Outside is death. We enter into that place of safety through Jesus. Any so-called freedom outside is short-sighted and short-lived.

Jesus is the door. And he is the only door. All are welcome to enter ('If *anyone*'), but they have to enter through him: 'If anyone enters *by me*'. He is the only door into that place of spiritual and eternal safety, and protection and life, because he alone is the Son of God who 'lays down his life for the sheep' (John 10:11).

Flawed designs

We'll explore this more in the chapter called 'I am the way', but Jesus' being the only door directly challenges two common ways of thinking, each of which can be pictured as a building.

The first building is a skyscraper. Sometimes, people seem to assume that humanity is living on the different floors of a moral skyscraper. On the top floor are the very best of people who work for hospitals and charities and give their lives to serving and caring for others. On the bottom floor are the casino owners, drug barons, arms dealers, and bankers. In the basement are the paedophiles. Most people put themselves on one of the middle floors, and they believe that God accepts all those on their floor and above. Very conveniently, everyone thinks that they just make the cut.

But Jesus is saying we're actually all on the same floor. It's a level playing field, we're all on it, and we're in terrible danger. There's only one way out of there and into the place of safety – and that's Jesus. It's not about different floors; it's about a door – and he is it.

The second misconception is represented by a building outside Chicago – a magnificent Baha'i temple. It's a circular construction with a huge dome. There are nine impressive doorways around the building that provide access. The nine doors open on to nine different aisles, which lead to a central place of worship; it's a wheel design. The doors are said to represent the nine major world religions. The idea is that no matter what our system of belief, we are all, in the end, united in worship together.

But Jesus doesn't say that he is one of nine doors and you can take your pick. He says that he is the *only* door. He's either spectacularly deluded or he's right. How do we know which?

He himself points to his 'works' – that is, his miracles – as the evidence that he is who he claims to be. He says, 'Even though you do not believe me, believe the works' (John 10:38). John's Gospel account documents them for us. John refers to them as 'signs', pointing to who Jesus is. Their purpose is 'that you may believe that Jesus is the Christ, the Son of God, and that by believing you may have life in his name' (John 20:31). They're worth checking out.

Abundant life

Jesus is the door to salvation, but salvation is not just *from* certain things. Salvation *for* what? Jesus says, 'I came that they may have life and have it abundantly' (John 10:10). He is the door to a life of abundance. He doesn't mean material abundance. He's not promising a life of perfect health, wealth, and prosperity. In fact, he teaches us to expect the opposite – that his followers will face much suffering in this life. What Jesus is promising here is a life of abundant spiritual provision.

Jesus develops the picture of the sheep and the sheepfold, saying, 'If anyone enters by me, he will be saved and will go in and out and find pasture' (10:9). It gives an idea of not just protection but also of pasture. It's a lovely image. Sheep protected by night and then, by day, being taken out to the best pasture where they can feed. Food for our souls – spiritual refreshment and nourishment.

It's the experience described by King David in one of the most well-known psalms:

> The LORD is my shepherd; I shall not want.
> He makes me lie down in green pastures.
> He leads me beside still waters.
> (Psalm 23:1–2)

In Jesus, we want for nothing; everything is provided. Our spiritual needs are met: our need for forgiveness, peace, purpose, and meaning.

The idea that God is stingy, a killjoy, and restrictive is a lie from the enemy, and it's an ancient one. Back at the beginning of human history, the devil, in the form of the serpent in the Garden of Eden, twisted God's words. He claimed that God had said the first people couldn't eat from any tree in the garden, when in fact God had said that they were free to eat from every tree except one.

God is a God of abundance, of generous, lavish, gracious provision. When the Old Testament prophets looked forward to what God was going to do in the future, when he would establish his kingdom, the images were of abundance:

And in that day
    the mountains shall drip sweet wine,
and the hills shall flow with milk.
(Joel 3:18)

The desert shall rejoice and blossom like
    the crocus;
it shall blossom abundantly
    and rejoice with joy and singing.
(Isaiah 35:1–2)

And that abundance is precisely what we see in the ministry of Jesus. For the first of his miracles, Jesus turned more than 600 litres of water into the best wine. He was making quite a statement, that he had come to bring life in abundance. In another of his signs, he turned five loaves and two fish into enough food for more than five thousand people. And there was so much to eat that, when the disciples were cleaning up, they filled twelve large baskets with leftovers.

The life Jesus promises is one of spiritual abundance, enjoyed in the fullness of the life to come but beginning now. The language of overflowing is used in the New Testament to speak of God's grace – his undeserved love and mercy. Through Jesus, we experience 'grace upon grace' (John 1:16); overflowing grace; 'the abundance of grace' (Romans 5:17); and 'the riches of his grace, which he lavished upon us' (Ephesians 1:7–8). Another verse speaks of the 'abundance of joy'

(2 Corinthians 8:2) that some of the early Christians experienced, despite extreme physical poverty.

God wants us not just to exist but to flourish; not just to survive but to thrive. This life comes through Jesus.

True freedom

This abundant life is also one of true freedom. Jesus says that we 'will go in and out and find pasture' (John 10:9). The sheep are not cooped up all day in a cage but, rather, are coming and going, grazing in the best pasture.

Is there restriction? Yes, in the sense that there is a shepherd who is in charge. And they have to follow him. Jesus said, 'If you keep my commandments, you will abide in my love' (John 15:10). But within that relationship, the sheep enjoy freedom and abundance because the shepherd is committed to their good.

The idea that freedom is the absence of any restriction whatsoever is widespread but mistaken. As someone has put it, 'Freedom is not so much the absence of restrictions as finding the right ones, the liberating restrictions.'[2] A fish is free only if it is restricted and limited to water. If you take a fish out of water and put it on the grass, you might think you're setting it free, but you're actually taking away its freedom to move and live. You're destroying it. So, as people, we are like fish that are designed to live in the water of knowing, obeying, serving, and loving God and others. That is our natural element; that is true freedom. It involves restrictions, but ones that set us free.

Take the example of marriage. Is the Bible's teaching on marriage restrictive? Yes, in that you are not free to have sex outside marriage. And within marriage, you're limiting yourself to just one person. You're tying yourself down. Closing off your options. Promising to be faithful until death. But that's the water within which we find true freedom. The people who say they want to be free to sleep around and do whatever, with whomever, whenever, are not really free. They're free like fish flopping around on the grass are free, gasping for air.

The same is true of friendship. Loving someone brings restrictions; it makes demands. But such loving relationships are like water for fish. To say you don't want that restriction, and you don't want to be answerable to anyone else, is to deny yourself one of life's greatest joys. It is to flop around on the grass.

God has made us for the water of knowing and loving him, and living that out in love for others. That is true freedom.

Rough ride

But such an abundant life may be one with considerable challenges. It may be a life in which we experience rejection from others for following Jesus.

One of those listening to Jesus' teaching was a blind man whom he had just healed. At one level, this man's life was harder now because of Jesus. The religious leaders had thrown him out of the synagogue and he'd been cast away from his community, but it was worth it for the joy of being able to see.

So, when people follow Jesus, they might experience opposition that they didn't have before, but they have the joy of being able to say with this man, 'I was blind but now I see' (spiritually speaking).

And the abundant life may have its fair share of other hardships and trials. That is a biblical pattern, confirmed by experience. In 1967, when she was in her late teens, Joni Eareckson Tada was involved in a diving accident that left her a quadriplegic, unable to move her hands or legs. It's been a desperately difficult journey, but she wrote on the fiftieth anniversary of the accident:

> I don't think you could find a happier follower of Jesus than me. The more my paralysis helps me get disentangled from sin, the more joy bubbles up from within. I can't tell you how many nights I have lain in bed, unable to move, stiff with pain, and have whispered near tears, 'Oh Jesus, I'm so happy. So very happy in you!'[3]

Here is abundant life even in the midst of suffering.

Enter here

Jesus said, 'I am the door. If anyone enters by me, he will be saved and will go in and out and find pasture . . . I came that they may have life and have it abundantly' (John 10:9, 10). It's a big claim and a gracious invitation, to anyone and everyone, to enter by him. Notice that it's not enough to just look at the door, admire the door, or hang around by the door. We need to enter. Personally. To go up to it, turn the handle, and walk through, putting our trust in Jesus.

I wonder how many doors you go through in the course of a day: the bathroom door, the front door, the door of a bus or a train; a shop door, workplace doors, or a gym door. Whenever you go through a door, why not ask yourself, 'Have I gone through this one? Have I entered through Jesus?'

It's as easy as opening a door and walking through, but it's also hard. It's hard when most other people are walking past the door and ignoring it, telling you not to bother. It's hard when going through that door may mean costly changes in thinking and living. Jesus knew that; he warned us, saying:

> Enter by the narrow gate. For the gate is wide and the way is easy that leads to destruction, and those who enter by it are many. For the gate is narrow and the way is hard that leads to life, and those who find it are few.
> (Matthew 7:13–14)

It's hard when life is so busy and we're tempted to procrastinate and put it off for another time – that mythical time when life is supposedly going to slow down. But Jesus cautioned us to 'strive to enter through the narrow door. For many, I tell you, will seek to enter and will not be able . . . once the master of the house has risen and shut the door' (Luke 13:24–25). When Jesus returns, the door into God's kingdom will be shut – for ever.

It's frustrating, isn't it, when you arrive at a bus stop just as the bus pulls away; even so, you have to wait only a few minutes for the next one. Perhaps you've arrived late for a flight and the gate was closed, but even then you can get on another flight. Imagine, though, if it were the last bus or the last flight, ever, to the kingdom of God and you'd missed it.

One day the door of salvation will be shut – for good. That is why the Bible urges us to enter through Jesus today, while there is still time.

I am THE GOOD SHEPHERD
John 10:11

Thank you for warning us in advance of your possible visit to our house to preach about your Sky Fairy. I'm sorry about your addiction to the evil that is religion, but I appreciate that you are prepared to warn people before you knock on their doors to spread your hatred. Please don't. Avoid our house.

So read the text sent to a church minister friend of mine. He had written to people in his area saying he'd like to come round. He provided an escape clause: if they didn't want a visit, they could text his number. The man's second text began with these words:

I was born Roman Catholic and forced to go to church every weekend. At Sunday school, the priest tried to make me [I'll spare you the details]. I didn't go again. I realized, aged 10, that this religion was evil. Just like all religions.

You can't blame him for drawing that conclusion. How many people today are like that poor guy, who have no time for God because of corrupt church leaders?

Someone dropped by our church the other day. We got chatting. He told me he'd been beaten black and blue as a schoolchild by nuns in Ireland. He wants nothing to do with God now, which is hardly surprising. I told that story to someone the next day and she said her mother had had the same experience – and the same reaction to God. And on it goes.

The cases that make the headlines are evidently just the tip of a very large iceberg. No wonder so many people have no time for God. Even if they haven't experienced such abuse themselves, they'll know others who have. Church leaders are supposed to represent God. If that is what God is like, then no thank you.

But that isn't what God is like at all. In fact, he is the very opposite. Jesus said, 'I am the good shepherd. The good shepherd lays down his life for the sheep' (John 10:11). There are bad shepherds out there who claim to represent God. They don't. If you want to know what God is like, look at Jesus, the good shepherd.

But what does Jesus mean when he says that he is the good shepherd? And how should we respond?

Ultimate sacrifice

In first-century Palestine, when Jesus spoke these words, sheep farming was everywhere, so the shepherd was a familiar figure. We've already heard Jesus describe himself as the door of the sheep-pen. Now the image switches to him as the shepherd. He uses this role as a picture of leadership. What kind of leader is Jesus? He's a good one: the good shepherd, who loves and cares for his people, the sheep he leads. He's the good shepherd who leaves the ninety-nine to go to search for the one that has gone astray.

But his goodness is seen, above all, in this: that 'the good shepherd lays down his life for the sheep'. He lays down his life on behalf of the sheep, not as an example to them but to rescue them from the danger they face.

Imagine a shepherd out with his sheep. He suddenly runs towards a cliff edge shouting, 'This is how much I love you,' and throws himself off, plunging to his death. How would that show his love for the sheep? It wouldn't. It would be pointless.

But now imagine instead that a wild animal was coming to attack the sheep. In the Old Testament, there was a shepherd boy called David (who later became a king). He wrote this:

> When there came a lion, or a bear, and took a lamb from the flock, I went after him and struck him and delivered it out of his mouth. And if he arose against me . . . I struck him and killed him.
> (1 Samuel 17:34–35)

That is the kind of scenario Jesus has in mind here.

If you want to update the picture, back in 2012, a gunman stormed a primary school in the USA. One of the teachers, 27-year-old Victoria Soto, sacrificed herself to save her pupils. Her final moments were spent ushering them into a closet when the gunman entered the classroom. She used her body to try to protect them and, by doing so, lost her life. She was found shot dead, huddled over her children. She had laid down her life for them.

So it is with Jesus. He laid down his life to save his people. He made the ultimate sacrifice. He died for them, to rescue them.

Real danger

What did Jesus rescue his people from? What was and is the danger? 'He who is a hired hand and not a shepherd, who does not own the sheep, sees the wolf coming and leaves the sheep and flees, and the wolf snatches them and scatters them' (John 10:12).

The reason some people have difficulty understanding why Jesus had to die for them is because they don't realize the danger they're in. There is a wolf coming and Jesus knew it, as we noted in the chapter 'I am the door'. One day we are going to die and face judgment. We are in terrible danger – eternal danger: 'it is appointed for man to die once, and after that comes judgement' (Hebrews 9:27). Jesus laid down his life to save us from the wolf of death and judgment. He took on himself the punishment we deserve for not going God's way. What love to do that for people like you and me!

Is that your picture of God? This is what God is like; the good shepherd is the God shepherd. In the Old Testament, God was often described as the shepherd of his people. Most famously in Psalm 23: 'The LORD is my shepherd.' For the Jewish people, the shepherd was God, so for Jesus to come along and claim to be *the* shepherd in *that* culture was to say that he was God become man.

What this means is that when we look at Jesus, we see what God is like – a loving, caring shepherd, who loves us so much that he sacrificed himself for us. So when we come across bad shepherds, corrupt leaders who claim to act in his name, we mustn't think God is like that. God is the exact opposite of the bad shepherd who exploits and abuses the sheep. But bad shepherds are out there, and Jesus himself warns us about them.

Hired hands

Jesus contrasts himself, as the good shepherd, with the 'hired hand':

> He who is a hired hand and not a shepherd, who does not own the sheep, sees the wolf coming and leaves the sheep and flees, and the wolf snatches and scatters them. He flees because he is a hired hand and cares nothing for the sheep.
> (John 10:12–13)

Jesus condemned the Jewish religious leaders of his day because they were like this. They didn't care for the sheep. They just cared for themselves. They were in it for what they could get – privilege, position, pay, and power. And they did nothing to protect the sheep from the wolf.

Sadly, there will be church leaders today who are just like that – who are in it for what they can get out of it. They don't warn the sheep about the wolf of death and judgment, and the need to be rescued through Jesus. Instead, they may just encourage people to try harder to be nice. But don't judge God by the hired hand. God isn't like that. In Jesus, he came as the good shepherd who loves the sheep. He loved them to death. He laid down his life for them.

Stop, thief!

Jesus also warned about those he called 'thieves and robbers': 'All who came before me are thieves and robbers, but the sheep did not listen to them . . . The thief comes only to steal and kill and destroy' (John 10:8, 10). He may have had in mind false messiahs. There were those, both before and after Jesus, who claimed to be the Messiah. Jesus warned that 'many will come in my name, saying "I am the Christ", and they will lead many astray' (Matthew 24:5). There have been many such people, down the ages, who have told people to follow them instead of Jesus, and who have damaged those who have done so.

People of this sort include cult leaders. For example, David Koresh led a cult in Waco, Texas, in which he abused the women, taking as his 'wives' girls as young as 12. In 1993, it all ended in a shoot-out with the authorities, resulting in the deaths of some seventy-five of his followers. Back in the 1970s, there was Jim Jones.

His cult ended with the forced mass suicide of 900 men, women and children in the South American rainforest, where they had gone to set up a paradisal community. Such leaders are thieves and robbers. They come only to steal and kill and destroy.

There have also been secular as well as religious messianic figures, and they exhibited the same disregard for life: Hitler, Stalin, Pol Pot, and Mao. These political 'saviours' slaughtered millions. People like these thieves and robbers steal – confiscating property; they kill – ruthlessly trampling lives underfoot; they destroy – savaging all that is valuable.

Cover-up

The thieves and robbers Jesus warned about also included lower-level, corrupt religious leaders. Jesus' teaching here (in John 10) follows straight on from a chapter in which the religious leaders of his day, the Pharisees, mistreated a blind man whom Jesus had just healed. The Pharisees were outwardly moral and respectable, but this was just a cover for every kind of wickedness, Jesus said. Similarly, today, there are corrupt church leaders who are thieves and robbers like them.

There are leaders who use religion as a cover for lust. They steal innocence. They kill faith. They destroy lives with their sexual abuse. Historic abuses within the Roman Catholic Church have dominated the headlines, but Protestant Churches are not immune from this either. An Australian friend told me of systematic sexual abuse that was uncovered in one diocese, among the senior leadership. In the UK, the Independent Enquiry into Child Sex Abuse published a report in 2020 which concluded that, over many years, the Church of England had created a culture where abusers could hide. In the USA, it would be a rare year without a high-profile pastor making the headlines because of a sex scandal. No country or church tradition is immune.

Then there are leaders who use religion as a cover for greed. They're out to steal your money. Jesse Duplantis, a US televangelist, claimed God had told him he needed a fourth private jet, so he called on people to donate the $54 million it would cost.[1] Also, in the history of the church, there have been leaders who have used religion as a justification for violence or for discrimination.

Thankfully not all are like this. Far from it. There are many godly, faithful church leaders, who are not perfect, because no-one is, but who are people of integrity. They know God and his transforming grace, and are seeking to live that out in changed lives. But there are bad shepherds, too; corrupt leaders, hired hands, and thieves and robbers. The point is that we mustn't make the mistake of thinking God is like that. He isn't.

God is as opposed to such corruption as any of us. In fact, much more so. One day he will judge people who do such terrible things in his name. In the meantime, the church should be committed to rooting out such corruption, not covering it up.

If you want to know what God is like, look at Jesus, the good shepherd – his love, his integrity, his self-sacrifice.

RSVP

We find three responses to Jesus in this chapter of John: reject, inspect, accept.

First, there are those who reject Jesus: 'Many of them said, "He has a demon, and is insane; why listen to him?"' (John 10:20). And before long they wanted to arrest him (10:39) and kill him (10:31).

Second, there are those who inspect Jesus and want to find out more: 'Others said, "These are not the words of one who is oppressed by a demon. Can a demon open the eyes of the blind?"' (10:21). Jesus' words and deeds are definitely worth a closer look. 'The works that I do in my Father's name bear witness about me,' Jesus said (10:25). He invites us to examine the evidence for ourselves.

And third, there are those who accept him: 'And many believed in him there' (10:42). These are his sheep. In the end, each of us will follow somebody. The question is simply who it's going to be. If not Jesus, then who? And how does what the other offers compare?

Benefits package

Look at what you get as one of *Jesus'* sheep.

Identity

Jesus' followers are God's true sheep. His flock. Jesus wasn't setting up a new cult. He is God the shepherd become man. His flock is God's flock. He said, 'So there will be one flock, one shepherd' (John 10:16). He is the leader of the one flock of God's true people. If we want to be part of that, we need to follow him.

Relationship

'My sheep hear my voice, and I know them, and they follow me' (10:27). What Jesus offers is not just signing up to a set of beliefs or joining a new club. It's about God in Christ knowing you personally and caring for you: 'he calls his own sheep by name' (10:3). It's about the Creator God knowing you by name.

Life

'I give them eternal life, and they will never perish' (10:28). Jesus gives his sheep eternal life. He rescues them from the wolf of death and judgment because he died in their place.

Security

No one will snatch them out of my hand. My Father, who has given them to me, is greater than all, and no one is able to snatch them out of the Father's hands. I and the Father are one. (10:28–30)

Many people feel insecure. They've no idea where they're going or what they're here for. They don't really feel they belong or that anyone loves them. Jesus offers security. Once you're in his hand, the Father's hand – Jesus and the Father are one – you are eternally safe. No-one has more power. You're protected from all the forces of evil.

So it's a good deal being part of his flock – you get identity, relationship, life, and security. But how do you join?

Voice recognition

'The sheep follow him, for they know his voice. A stranger they will not follow, but they will flee from him, for they do not know the voice of strangers' (John 10:4–5). There are lots of different voices in the world saying, 'Follow me. Come my way.' Amid the noise, Jesus' sheep recognize the voice of the good shepherd. They recognize Jesus' voice as God's voice. So a good place to start is to read through John's Gospel and ask God to help you to recognize God himself speaking to you in Jesus.

That initial response to his voice is a continuing mark of God's true sheep. They keep listening to Jesus and seek to obey his teaching; that is, they follow him: 'The sheep follow him, for they know his voice' (10:4). Being a Christian is about following Jesus Christ through life. It's about knowing him, listening to him and his teaching, obeying him, and serving him. Doing so shapes how we live.

Corrupt church leaders prove by their lifestyles that they themselves aren't actually Jesus' sheep. If they were, they would follow him and live differently. They're frauds. Counterfeits – and poor ones at that.

At the bottom of one of the many online articles about corrupt church leaders, someone left this comment: 'Not much goodness left in today's religion. Just greed and lust.' Well, Jesus did warn about thieves and robbers masquerading as church leaders, people who use religion as a cloak for greed and lust. But we mustn't judge God by such counterfeits and reject God on their account. Such people don't speak for him. They don't represent him. They're nothing like him.

The fact that there are corrupt politicians and dictators in the world doesn't mean we reject politics or government. The fact that there is counterfeit money in circulation doesn't mean we stop using cash. The fact that there are fake paintings doesn't mean we stop visiting galleries. A museum in France, dedicated to the painter Étienne Terrus, discovered that more than half its paintings were forgeries. A committee of experts confirmed that 82 of the 140 works were not painted by the artist, who was a close friend of Henri Matisse. It's been estimated that at least 20% of all the paintings held by major galleries are fake. Do you give up on art because of it? No. You expose the fakes and focus on the genuine.

So it is with Christianity. Look for the true, the genuine, the good. Jesus said, 'I am the good shepherd. The good shepherd lays down his life for the sheep.' He calls us to hear his voice and follow him.

I am THE RESURRECTION

John 11:25

My mother died today.

I must have been 18 when I first read that opening sentence of Albert Camus' novel *The Stranger*. It haunted me from then on – the thought that the day would come when I would have to say the same.

It didn't happen for another thirty years but, when it did, it was fully as hard as I had imagined. And there was no time to sit together and reflect on life and say everything you wanted to say. With both my mum and my dad, it was very sudden. Just a phone call from someone saying that they'd died. The death of loved ones is such a painful part of life, as so many of us know from experience.

Then, on top of that, you've got the prospect of your own death. Freud was on to something when he wrote, 'No one believes in his own death.'[1] Death, we think, is what happens to other people. But it will come to all of us, sooner or later. Perhaps sooner than we think.

Some cope by joking about it, like Woody Allen, who said, 'I'm not afraid of death. I just don't want to be there when it happens.'[2] Others use euphemisms to soften the harsh reality. They speak of 'moving on' or 'passing away'. Some refuse to speak about death at all. It's the taboo subject. The elephant in the room.

Death haunts us. We feel helpless. It's like a tyrant who can't be stopped. A monster that destroys everything in its path. An undefeated heavyweight boxing champion who is simply too strong. A bully in the playground who is too big. If only there were someone who had the power to stand up to him, to take death on and defeat him, to save us from him. But who would dare to claim he or she had that kind of power?

Jesus did. It's one of the many things that make him so compelling. Standing at the grave of a friend, he declared, 'I am the resurrection and the life. Whoever believes in me, though he die, yet shall he live, and everyone who lives and believes in me shall never die' (John 11:25–26).

What did he mean? And why should we believe him?

Beyond the grave

The first part of Jesus' astonishing claim is that he is 'the resurrection'. He explains the significance of this as 'whoever believes in me, though he die, yet shall he live' (John 11:25). As the resurrection, Jesus promises life beyond the grave for those who trust in him. To prevent misunderstanding, it might be worth beginning with what he doesn't mean.

First, he's not just talking about your reputation or influence living on after you. One author wrote:

> Like everyone who finds existence interesting and occasionally enjoyable, I want to live for ever. And I'm pretty sure that I won't. The best I can do is to see that my genes live on through my children, and that my thoughts live on through my writing.[3]

But that's not what Jesus is talking about – achieving so-called immortality through physical procreation or artistic creation. It's not just a case of 'Fame! I'm gonna live for ever!', as the theme song of the old TV series declared. Jesus is talking about life actually continuing beyond death.

Second, he doesn't just mean living on after death spiritually. He means physically. The Bible teaches that those who trust in Jesus go to be with him in spirit the moment they die. But that is just a stop on the journey, not the destination. The destination is the resurrection of the body to live in a renewed universe; to be raised, one day, to a life as physical as the one we now enjoy but infinitely better. With bodies that will never get sick or old or die, we will live in a world in which there is no evil or suffering.

The word 'cemetery' comes from a Greek word that means 'dormitory'. A dormitory is a sleeping-room with several beds. That's what a cemetery is, a sleeping place for the body, which, one day, will be woken up by Jesus for life with him.

Third, Jesus doesn't just mean resuscitation. Resuscitation is when you revive someone, bringing them back to life, but they later die again at some point.

54

Resurrection is different. It's being raised to a new, eternal, indestructible life, never to die again. That's what Jesus is promising: we're gonna live for ever – literally.

The Alcor Life Extension Foundation in Arizona is the world leader in cryonics. Cryonics is the science of using ultra-cold temperature to preserve dead human bodies, with the intention of restoring good health to those bodies, when the technology becomes available to do so, and reviving them. Basically, when you die, the cryonics scientists put your brain, or your whole body, in a deep freeze of liquid nitrogen, with the hope that at some point, in years to come, they'll find a cure for the illness that nobbled you and discover a way of reversing the freezing process safely. At the time of writing, Alcor has 162 patients in the deep freeze. You can join them for a mere $200,000.

It's bold stuff, but no-one at Alcor is claiming that they might one day be able to keep you alive for ever. The best they can hope for is life extension, as highlighted in the name of the company. By contrast, Jesus is promising resurrection to life for ever.

Fourth, it's not automatic. 'I am the resurrection . . . whoever believes in me, though he die, yet shall he live' (John 11:25). The invitation is open to all – it's for 'whoever'. Yet the condition is clear: 'whoever believes in me'. All are not just automatically raised to life with Jesus.

When someone dies, the loved ones who are left often say things such as 'At least so-and-so is now at peace and in a better place', even if so-and-so had nothing to do with Jesus when he or she was alive. It's assuming every-one qualifies for what Jesus promises, whether or not they have trusted in him.

Jesus, though, says otherwise. The necessity of per-sonal faith is a recurring theme in John's Gospel:

> For God so loved the world, that he gave his only Son, that whoever *believes in him* should not perish but have eternal life . . . Whoever *believes in the Son* has eternal life; whoever does not obey the Son shall not see life, but the wrath of God remains on him.
> (John 3:16, 36)

Second death

The second part of Jesus' claim is that he is the life. He explains what this means as 'everyone who lives and believes in me shall never die' (John 11:26).

As a church minister, I've officiated at many a funeral. Walking down the aisle of a church filled with mourners, ahead of a coffin, proclaiming in a loud voice that Jesus said 'everyone who lives and believes in me shall never die' can feel rather awkward. It seems so patently false. Christians do die, just like everyone else. The body is in the coffin. The person is dead. That's why it's a funeral.

So did Jesus get it wrong? Or is there a sense in which those who believe in him never die? He didn't, and, yes, there is. Physically, followers of Jesus die like everyone else, but the Bible talks about a 'second death'. This language is used of the eternal judgment, to which all of us, by nature, are heading, for not living with God as God in our lives:

> This is the second death, the lake of fire.
> (Revelation 20:14)

> The lake that burns with fire and sulphur, which is the second death.
> (21:8)

The second death is a much bigger problem than the first death. It is from this second death that those who trust in Jesus are rescued.

Eternal life

Why does Jesus promise this to 'everyone who lives and believes in' him (John 11:26)? It seems an odd, and unnecessary, thing to say. Of course, you have to live to believe in him!

Probably what Jesus means by 'lives' is 'lives spiritually', not just physically; that is, 'lives' in the sense of having eternal life through believing in him. He's indicating that eternal life begins even now for those who trust in Jesus.

'Truly, truly, I say to you, whoever hears my word and believes him who sent me *has* eternal life. He does not come into judgement, but *has passed* from death to life', Jesus said (John 5:24). If we believe in Jesus, we have already crossed over from death to life. Eternal life, which is relationship with God through Jesus, has already begun.

So Jesus is promising not just life after death but life before death as well. Without this eternal life now, we're just existing, not enjoying the fullness of life for which God made us. As someone has put it, albeit rather cornily, Jesus is not just offering pie in the sky when you die but also steak on your plate while you wait! Life after death but life before death, too.

'I am the resurrection and the life. Whoever believes in me, though he die, yet shall he live, and everyone who lives and believes in me shall never die. Do you believe this?' (John 11:25–26). That's the question Jesus put to a woman called Martha. And it's a question he puts to us today. Do you believe this? Do you believe him?

Martha sort of believed, but not fully. Others might say, 'I'd like to believe this. It sounds wonderful. But I'm not gullible. I need evidence. Where's the proof Jesus can deliver? Too much is riding on this to just cross my fingers and hope for the best.' It's a good question – the right question.

Stake your claim

'Stake Your Claim' is a classic 1970s TV comedy sketch from *Monty Python's Flying Circus*. A game-show host interviews various individuals who have made big claims. First up is Mr Voles of Gravesend, who claims to have written all the works usually attributed to

Shakespeare. The host asks, 'Mr Voles, these plays are known to have been performed in the early seventeenth century. How old are you?'

'Forty-three,' he answers.

'Well,' the host continues, 'how is it possible for you to have written plays performed over three hundred years before you were born?'

'Ah, well,' Mr Voles replies, 'this is where my claim falls to the ground. There's no possible way of answering that argument, I'm afraid. I was only hoping you would not make that particular point, but I can see you're more than a match for me!'

A claim, to be credible, needs evidence. Jesus' claim to be the resurrection and the life, unlike that of Mr Voles, stands up to examination. Jesus made his claim at a funeral, and to prove that he could deliver, he raised the dead man, Lazarus, to life.

The FAQs section of the Alcor website includes one very revealing question: 'Has anyone ever been revived?' Answer: 'No adult human has ever been revived from temperatures far below freezing. This technology may become a reality a century or more in the future.' The game's up. There's no hard evidence to back up the speculation. By contrast, Jesus gave a physical and public demonstration of his power to make good on his promise.

Dead and buried

John's record of the raising of Lazarus in his Gospel account is historically reliable. It was written by someone at the time, an eyewitness, a person of integrity, who was committed to telling the truth, and who had nothing to gain from making it up. It is an account that was circulating during the lifetimes of other eyewitnesses, many of whom were hostile. It has been faithfully and accurately passed down to us. This trustworthy report makes it clear that Lazarus was most definitely dead.

Note the explicit expressions: 'Martha, the sister of the dead man . . . The man who had died' (John 11:39, 44).

Note the time in the tomb: 'Now when Jesus came, he found that Lazarus had already been in the tomb four days' (11:17). Lazarus was dead and buried. Not only had he been in there for four days but his hands and feet had also been 'bound with linen strips, and his face wrapped with a cloth' (11:44).

Note the many mourners: 'many of the Jews had come to Martha and Mary to console them concerning their brother' (11:19). The account highlights their intense grief (11:33). There was no doubt in any of their minds that Lazarus was dead.

Note the concern about nasty niffs: Martha says, 'Lord, by this time there will be an odour, for he has been dead four days' (11:39). One older translation puts it rather graphically, 'Lord, by this time he stinketh' (KJV). You can imagine what it was like in the hot climate of Palestine. Her fear about the smell of decomposition was understandable, and was a clear sign that she knew her brother was dead.

Charles Dickens begins the story of *A Christmas Carol* by saying, 'There is no doubt that Marley was dead. This must be distinctly understood, or nothing wonderful can come of the story I am going to relate.' And that is the case also with this true story. We need to understand that Lazarus was most definitely dead, or there is nothing wonderful in what happens next.

Raised to life

Lazarus was definitely raised to life.

Note the powerful proclamation: Jesus 'cried out with a loud voice, "Lazarus come out." The man who died came out, his hands and feet bound with linen strips, and his face wrapped with a cloth' (John 11:43–44).

Note the enemies' reaction: 'So the chief priests and the Pharisees gathered the Council and said, "What are we to do? For this man performs many signs. If we let him go on like this, everyone will believe in him"' (11:47–48). If even his enemies acknowledged the miracle, that's strong evidence. And how could they deny it? It was a public event, witnessed by a large crowd: 'The crowd that been with him when he called Lazarus out of the tomb and raised him from the dead continued to bear witness' (John 12:17).

Note the thanksgiving celebration: 'Six days before the Passover, Jesus . . . came to Bethany, where Lazarus was, whom Jesus had raised from the dead. So they gave a dinner for him there' (12:1–2). What a dinner that must have been, in Jesus' honour, and with Lazarus actually there eating with them. Lots of jokes, no doubt, at Lazarus' expense – 'Tuck in Laz, you haven't eaten for days', and the like!

Note the tourist attraction:

> When the large crowd of the Jews learned that Jesus was there, they came, not only on account of him, but also to see Lazarus, whom he had raised from the dead. So the chief priests made plans to put Lazarus to death as well, because on account of him many of the Jews were going away and believing in Jesus.
> (12:9–11)

Bethany was just two miles from Jerusalem, so this was a gift of a day-trip from the capital. Many came, saw, and believed.

Does it seem too much to believe in such a miracle in the twenty-first century? Back in the first century, they would have been as sceptical as people today. But they were convinced by what they saw; by the evidence. Lazarus was definitely raised from the dead. It was a demonstration by Jesus of his power over death.

Final proof

The ultimate proof, though, that Jesus is the resurrection and the life is the death and resurrection of Jesus himself, which John records in his final chapters. As with the one about Lazarus, the account is clear: Jesus was definitely dead – flogged, crucified, dead, and buried – but definitely raised.

His resurrection on the Sunday was as historical and real as his crucifixion on the Friday. If you'd been there on the Friday, you could have rubbed your hand on the cross and got a splinter. If you'd been there on the Sunday, you could have gone into the tomb and seen that it was empty. All that remained were the grave-clothes in which Jesus had been buried, lying there, undisturbed, his body having passed through them.

Exhibit A is the empty tomb. That's the first piece of evidence. The second is his resurrection appearances. Over a forty-day period, Jesus appeared to lots of different people, at different times, in different places. These two bits of evidence, fulfilling what the Old Testament and Jesus himself had foretold, left those early followers utterly convinced that Jesus had been raised to life – so convinced that they were prepared to die for it.

On one occasion when Jesus appeared to his disciples, they thought he was a ghost. But Jesus then did the ghost test. It's worth giving it a go yourself. If you wake up in the middle of the night and see someone at the foot of your bed, you'll probably want to find out whether or not what you see is a ghost. How do you do that? There are two simple tests.

First, the touch test. Reach out and touch the person. If your hand hits something solid – flesh and bone – that's not a ghost. That's a living human. Second, there's the food test. Give the nocturnal visitor something to eat: a chocolate bar, a biscuit, or a full, cooked meal – it doesn't matter what. If food disappears when it goes into the individual's mouth, the person is not a ghost. A ghost doesn't have an oesophagus, intestines, and a stomach.

These are precisely the tests that Jesus encouraged his disciples to use when he appeared to them and they thought that he was a ghost. He said to them:

> 'Touch me, and see. For a spirit does not have flesh and bones as you see that I have ... Have you anything here to eat?' They gave him a piece of broiled fish, and he took it and ate before them. (Luke 24:39, 41–43)

Disappearing daffodils

Jeremy Cooke – or Mr Justice Cooke, to give him his title – is a former high court judge. For a short two-week trial, he might have had twenty to twenty-five lever-arch files of evidence to read through and assess; for a commercial case with multinational companies, between 150 and 200 files. So, he's used to examining evidence; it's what he's done for a living. He says, 'Law is based on the premise that truth is discoverable from evidence.'[4]

When he gives a talk on the evidence for the resurrection of Jesus, he tends to begin by eating a daffodil (as you do), and he says this:

> Imagine going back to your flat and telling your mates that you've just seen a high court judge eat a daffodil. They might not believe you. But what if

twenty or five hundred people reported the same, and they were people of integrity?

The evidence is what people say they've seen and heard. You need to evaluate it, look at contrary evidence, and work out what is the most coherent explanation. That is precisely what we have to do with the resurrection of Jesus.[5]

That's what Jeremy has done and he is persuaded that the evidence points in only one direction – that Jesus really was raised to life.

He was raised for ever. Jesus raised Lazarus to life but, at some point, Lazarus would die again. There would be a second funeral. But Jesus was raised for ever. He defeated death.

Perhaps think of it in terms of tennis. Death was like a world-class tennis player who was undefeated. Whomever he had played throughout history, it had been game, set, and match to Death. With Lazarus, Death had lost a set but then had come back to win the match. But Jesus, by his resurrection, defeated Death. It was the first time ever that Death lost. When Jesus was dead and buried, it looked as if Death had won but, as he burst out of the tomb, Jesus clinched the match – the greatest comeback of all time!

The black cloth

One day each of us will die. Who are you going to trust with your own death? A deep-freeze outfit in Arizona or Jesus Christ, whose qualifications include the raising of Lazarus and his own conquest of death?

Jim Rohn is a motivational guru whose philosophy has, apparently, helped millions of people to improve their business and personal lives, leadership skills, and finances. Presumably, along the way, it has improved his own finances a teeny bit as well. One of his bestselling books is called *The Keys to Success*. That's all well and good, but it's not going to be much help to any of us when we're staring death in the face.

Imagine yourself, one day, in a care home with weeks to live. Would you be thankful if someone gave you a copy of Jim's book? We don't just need someone who can get us through life successfully – we need someone who can get us through death and bring us out into life on the other side. In the end, we need more than Jim. We need Jesus.

Picture death as a piece of black cloth. Jesus is like a needle that pierces the cloth and comes out the other side. If we trust in him, we are like the thread in the eye of the needle. One day we will be pulled through the hole that Christ has made and out into life with him on the other side – if we are joined to him through faith.

At the back of the graveyard of a village church, not far from the English Lake District, is a simple headstone. Engraved on it are the words of Jesus: 'I am the resurrection and the life', followed by the names Jonathan and Esther Nodder. My brothers and I chose this verse for Mum and Dad's grave because it sums up why we are convinced that death is not the end, and that we will see them again.

Many a time, as a church minister taking a funeral, I've read these lines at a graveside:

> We now commit *his/her* body to the grave in the sure and certain hope of the resurrection to eternal life for all who trust in Christ, who will change our frail and mortal bodies to be like his glorious resurrection body.[6]

The hope is 'sure and certain' because of Jesus.

The question Jesus put to Martha, he puts to each one of us: 'Do you believe this?' We have every reason to. And we need to, if we are to enjoy the life he promises.

I am THE WAY

John 14:6

I was chatting to a neighbour and we got on to the subject of religion. Her mother is Roman Catholic and her father Buddhist. She herself married a Muslim, with whom she has a young child who has been baptized into the Roman Catholic Church, but is also being brought up as a Muslim.

Here in the UK, as in many Western countries, there is such a mix of cultures and religions, even in the same family. According to the 2011 population census, the London borough of Tower Hamlets, in which I live, is 38% Muslim and 30% Christian; 21% claim to have no religion; and the remaining 11% follow other religions or are categorized as 'religion not stated'. It makes London a fascinating place to be, but it also brings challenges – especially for followers of Jesus.

Jesus said, 'I am the way, and the truth, and the life. No one comes to the Father except through me' (John 14:6). The 'I am' sayings of Jesus are all extraordinary, but this one really turns up the heat.

A US church pastor called Tim Keller says:

> During my nearly two decades in New York City, I've had numerous opportunities to ask people,

'What is your biggest problem with Christianity? What troubles you the most about its beliefs or how it is practised?' One of the most frequent answers I've heard over the years can be summed up in one word: 'exclusivity'.[1]

He's referring to Jesus' claim to be the only way. What exactly does Jesus mean?

Homesick for heaven

If someone said to you, 'I am the way,' the obvious response would be: 'The way to where? To what?' So it is here. Jesus is the way, but what is the destination? He tells us: 'In my Father's house are many rooms. If it were not so, would I have told you that I go to prepare a place for you?' (John 14:2). Jesus says that he is the way to his Father's house – that is, to heaven. He speaks of coming 'to the Father' (14:6). He is the way to God the Father; to heaven – and to life there with God.

'How do I get to heaven?' This question is monumentally important. The Bible assures us that death is not the end. Jesus taught that when we die, either we will go to be with God in heaven or we will be alienated from him and his goodness in hell. 'How do I get to heaven?' is a question that we should all be asking. But if you're not, before dismissing any such talk as being of no concern, consider for a moment the possibility that you may actually be more interested in heaven than you think.

When I was young and single, I spent a couple of weeks backpacking round South East Asia on my own. It seemed like a great idea at the time, but it didn't take long for me to feel very homesick. I got food poisoning and ended up in a cheap hostel somewhere, with a severe case of diarrhoea and vomiting, longing to be home. I was sick, lonely, and out of place. All of us will have had some experience of feeling homesick.

But G. K. Chesterton wrote, 'Men are homesick in their homes.'[2] There is a deeper homesickness: a cosmic, spiritual homesickness. You can feel it even when you're at home. It's a feeling that you're not really at home in life. You feel like a stranger on your own planet; alienated, as if your true home were elsewhere. How do we explain this feeling? Where does this cosmic homesickness come from, if this is all there is and if what we see is what we get?

The Bible's explanation makes a lot of sense – we're homesick for heaven because that is our true home. We were made by God for God. Heaven is the home we long for, without realizing that's what we're missing.

Sigmund Freud would, of course, say that heaven is just something we've invented because we have a desire for a heavenly father figure to look after us and to go somewhere when we die. But where has this desire come from? Why do we have it? It's very hard to explain if we're nothing but electro-chemical machines or high-functioning animals.

C. S. Lewis wrote:

> Creatures are not born with desires unless satisfaction for those desires exists. A baby feels hunger: well, there is such a thing as food. A duckling wants to swim: well, there is such a thing as water. Men feel sexual desire: well, there is such a thing as sex. If I find in myself a desire which no experience in this world can satisfy, the most probable explanation is that I was made for another world.[3]

Route map

Jesus says that the way to our true home, to heaven with God, is him – Jesus: 'I am the way.' It's a bold, outrageous claim: not 'I can show you the way' but 'I am the way'. His claim is vindicated, though, by who he is and what he's done. 'I am the way, and the truth, and the life,' he said (John 14:6). It is because he is the truth and the life that he is the way.

He is the truth – the supreme revelation of God: 'grace and truth came through Jesus Christ' (John 1:17). He makes God known to us because he is one with the Father: 'Whoever has seen me has seen the Father' (John 14:9). This means that there is no real truth about God, the world, or ourselves apart from Jesus.

I was working out one day, watching an exercise video, when an advert popped up for an online masterclass with the world-renowned astrophysicist Neil deGrasse Tyson. He's one of the most popular figures in modern science, with a hit talk show and bestselling books. In the trailer for this masterclass on how to think, he says:

> I've come to realize that there are three categories of truth – personal truths, political truths, and objective truths that shape our understanding of the universe. The interesting thing about an objective truth is that it's true no matter what. The good thing about science is that it's true whether or not you believe it.[4]

In which category would you put God? A common approach nowadays is to assign anything to do with God to the personal truth box. Belief in him is seen as nothing more than your personal opinion. Just true for you, not objectively true in the way that $2 + 2 = 4$ or that the sun is 150 million kilometres from Earth. But Jesus is claiming here to be the Truth with a capital 'T'. Objective truth. True no matter what. True whether or not you believe it.

And he is the life. 'In him was life' (John 1:4). Through him, we come to experience this life for ourselves – eternal life. And it begins now. Through Jesus, we go home to God in heaven one day but, even now, God comes to make his home with us, and in us, through the Holy Spirit. 'If anyone loves me, he will keep my word, and my Father will love him, and we will come to him and make our home with him' (John 14:23).

So, Jesus is the way because of who he is – the truth and the life. But he's the way also because of what he's done. Jesus twice says to the disciples, 'I go to prepare a place for you' (14:2, 3). Does he mean that he's going to get heaven ready and give it a good clean? Is it that they've been rather short-staffed in heaven, leaving his Father's house in a bit of a mess, so that he has to go to get things sorted – that he has to change the sheets and sweep the floors?

No, what he's saying is that his death on the cross will prepare a place in heaven for his people. That's *how* he was going. He was about to leave them, to die on the cross, be raised to life, and return to heaven, from where he would send the Holy Spirit. All of that would prepare a place in heaven for his people.

It is his going, in death and resurrection, paying for our sins, that makes it possible for any of us to go to heaven. Jesus became homeless here in this life and was abandoned by his Father on the cross, for us, so that we might come home to the Father.

One way

So, the destination is heaven, and the route there is Jesus. 'I am the way, and the truth, and the life.' And because he is the truth and the life, he is the only way. He goes on to say, 'No one comes to the Father except through me' (John 14:6). There is only one way and he is it – because of who he is and what he's done.

No-one gets to heaven, to God, except through Jesus. Not you, not me, not anyone. No exceptions. No-one gets there through living a good life, by doing their best, by attending church, or by following whatever religion – only through Jesus. He's the only bridge between us and God: 'there is salvation in no one else, for there is no other name under heaven given among men by which we must be saved' (Acts 4:12). Heaven is open to all, but Jesus is the only way in.

Aron Ralston was climbing alone in the narrow Blue-john Canyon in Utah, when a dislodged 360-kilogram boulder fell on his right arm, trapping him against a rock. He had just one litre of water, no mobile phone, and hadn't told anyone where he was going. Not good. Five days into his ordeal it struck him that there was only one way he was going to make it out alive – and it involved his arm and a cheap, blunt pocketknife. If you're squeamish, you may want to skip the next few lines.

He managed to puncture the skin of his arm, but quickly realized that without a saw he wasn't going to get through bone. So, he flung himself against the boulder to break his arm, and then spent the next hour hacking through his flesh. Once through, he used pieces of climbing kit to make a tourniquet to stop himself bleeding to death, and somehow managed to scale a 20-metre cliff to get out of the canyon. He was eventually picked up by a search-and-rescue helicopter. The film *127 Hours* tells his story.

That Aron subjected himself to such unimaginable horror and pain tells us one thing very clearly – there was no other way out. If there had been, he would never have done this to himself. So it is with Jesus. If there were any other way for us to get right with God, do we really think he would have sent his Son into this world, to endure the horror of torture and execution on a cross, with all the suffering that involved – physical agony, spiritual desolation, and social rejection?

Some would say that such an exclusive view – that Jesus is the only way – is dangerous, divisive, and a threat to peace. But Christians, if they obey what Jesus teaches, will not be forcing anyone to believe as they do. Christians are to spread the message through love, and with gentleness and respect. They are to follow the example of Jesus himself, who died for his enemies, praying for the Father to forgive them.

So, it's perfectly possible to believe this exclusive claim and also live peaceably alongside those of different beliefs. Three of my children attend a Muslim-majority school. All their schoolmates are Muslim. They have some frank exchanges of views but they're still friends.

Mountains and elephants

In today's culture, though, the exclusive claims of Jesus are more likely to provoke hostility not from the religious person but from the secular individual. Consider some of the slogans of the modern Western, secular outlook: 'All religions lead to the same destination,' it claims. 'They're just different paths up the same mountain. So it's arrogant to claim your religion is right and to try to convert others to it.' (We've touched on this briefly already in the chapter entitled 'I am the door'.) But to assert that all paths lead to the same destination is surely the ultimate in arrogance. Such a person is claiming that they alone can see where all the paths lead, they alone know better than the followers of these different religions; they are right and everyone must agree with them.

The fact is that each one of us believes that his or her view is the right one, so accusations of arrogance don't get us very far. The key questions are which position *is* right and which claim stands up? And they require that we examine the evidence and weigh it up.

Another slogan of the secular relativist is that 'everyone just has a part of the truth'. The story is told of a king with an elephant. He ordered six blind men to be brought in to him. He asked each of them to describe what was in front of them. One described a tail that he was holding, another a leg, another a trunk, another an ear, and another a fold of skin. So, it is claimed, each of the world religions has a grasp of just part of the truth about spiritual reality, but none of them can see the whole elephant. Conveniently, the person who argues this is assuming that he or she is the king in the story – the only one who is not blind! Why should we believe this individual's exclusive claim? Where's the evidence?

Sincerely wrong

Another slogan is, 'As long as you are sincere, God will accept you.' But being sincere and being right are very different things. It is possible to be sincerely wrong. Hitler was sincere and convinced that it was right to kill millions of Jews, but he was wrong. Or, to take a more everyday example, if you're on a plane, it doesn't matter how sincere you are in your belief that you're heading to Sydney, if in fact your flight is en route to San Francisco. The sincerity of your belief doesn't change reality, and so it is spiritually.

Another slogan is that 'Christ will save everyone'. This claim that sincere followers of other religions will be saved through Christ, although they don't trust in him, is a view that you even find in some church circles. But the followers of these religions would be highly offended to be told that they were in fact Christians without being aware of it – so-called 'anonymous Christians'.

When Jesus says that we get to heaven only through him, he means through faith in him: 'Believe . . . in me,' he says (John 14:1). His comment that in his Father's house are 'many rooms' (14:2) is sometimes used to argue that in heaven there's a room for each religion. In fact, all Jesus means is that there is plenty of room for anyone and everyone who believes in him.

A final objection people raise is that it's not fair of God to reject people for not believing in a Jesus of whom they've never heard. But the Bible makes it clear that people who've never heard of Jesus will be held to account by God for rejecting the light they've had, not for rejecting a Jesus of whom they are ignorant.

What this means, though, is that in order to be saved, people do need to hear the message about Jesus; that is why Christian organizations, churches, and individuals are doing everything they can to get the message of Jesus to the world, in obedience to his command to 'go therefore and make disciples of all nations' (Matthew 28:19).

No way

Jesus says there is only one way. The secular relativist says there are many ways.

Finally, sceptics say there is no way. As mentioned at the beginning of this chapter, 21% of people in our London borough said that they were of 'no religion' in the last population census. Such people tend to see all religions as just a product of a particular culture, and so not true. They say things such as 'If you were born in Morocco, you're likely to be Muslim. If you were born in Malawi, you're likely to be Christian.'

But the sceptics have to recognize that if all views are just a product of culture, then that applies to their view as well, so we shouldn't listen to them either. But, actually, what is striking about Christianity is how it transcends cultures. It's all over the world. It has taken root in every country and culture.

You choose

Jesus said, 'I am the way, and the truth, and the life. No one comes to the Father except through me' (John 14:6). Either Jesus is right, in which case we'd be fools to ignore him, or he's wrong, in which case he can't be the good man or wise teacher that some claim. Instead, he would be a liar or a lunatic. The question is this: which conclusion really fits the facts?

C. S. Lewis wrote:

> A man who was merely a man and said the sort of things Jesus said would not be a great moral teacher. He would either be a lunatic – on the level with the man who says he is a poached egg – or else he would be the Devil of Hell. You must make your choice. Either this man was, and is, the Son of God, or else a madman or something worse.
>
> You can shut him up for a fool, you can spit at him and kill him as a demon, or you can fall at his feet and call him Lord and God, but let us not come with any patronizing nonsense about his being a great human teacher. He has not left that open to us. He did not intend to.[5]

Like many people, Caroline Clarke had put Jesus in precisely the box that Lewis says is not an option. She thought she knew what Christianity was about and she wasn't interested. She studied other religions and travelled the world to see them at work. Caroline was genuinely seeking truth but, she said, 'Christianity really was the last place I looked because I assumed that I knew what it was.' At 25, she moved from the UK to Australia. One Sunday evening, while recovering from a hangover, she was at a loose end and wandered into a local church. The people there invited her for a week-end conference in the Blue Mountains. Bush-walking sounded fun, so she went along. For the first time – as she listened to someone teaching the Bible – she found herself questioning assumptions that she had made about herself and about Jesus. 'I'd grown up thinking that I was a pretty OK person, and that I had always tried to do the right thing by everybody. I thought God knew my intentions, and that would be good enough for him.' But she was challenged by the truth that if you've missed the bus, you've missed the bus, regardless by how much. She had also assumed that Jesus was just a good teacher who had died an unjust death. She came to see, though, that this simply didn't fit with what he claimed and that she needed to take a closer look at him. These were her first steps towards following Jesus for herself.

Given the way the cultural winds are blowing, those who do accept Jesus' claim are going to find them-selves increasingly marginalized. But such hostility is nothing new. Jesus was killed for his exclusive teaching, so his followers should, at the very least, expect some push-back.

But it's worth putting up with being rejected and an outsider now, if it means you are accepted by God and have a home in heaven for eternity. Jesus said, 'I am the way, and the truth and the life. No one comes to the Father except through me.'

I am THE VINE

John 15:5

I'm a 46 year old banker . . . In a steady 9–7 job. 6 days a week. For 26 years . . . Today I found out that my wife has been cheating on me for the last 10 years. My son feels nothing for me. I realized I missed my father's funeral FOR NOTHING . . . I remember getting calls from Mom, telling me he was getting sicker and sicker. I was getting busier and busier, on the verge of a big promotion. I kept putting my visit off, hoping he would hold on. He died, and I got my promotion. I [hadn't] seen him in 15 years.

When he died, I told myself it didn't matter [that] I didn't see him. Being an atheist, I rationalized that [his] being dead, it wouldn't matter anyway. WHAT WAS I THINKING? . . . I regret letting my job take over my life. I regret being an awful husband, a money-making machine . . . Do NOT waste your life.[1]

This is the impassioned plea of a man called John Jerryson.

'YOLO', people say – You Only Live Once. This isn't a dry-run. This is it. So, we all want to make the most of it. But how? How do we make our lives count? What is a successful life?

An infographic chart by Anna Vital called 'Lost in Life?'[2] gives examples of people who took an indirect route to success. The actor and producer Harrison Ford was a carpenter until his thirties. J. K. Rowling was a single mum on benefits until the age of 31. The founder of McDonald's was selling paper cups and milkshake mixers until the age of 52. Harland Sanders didn't start Kentucky Fried Chicken (KFC) until he was 65. The message is – don't give up just because you're not successful at the moment; it's still possible; these people didn't achieve success until this or that age.

What is success, according to such thinking? It's about achievement at work; career success. It's drummed into us from the earliest age that this is success in life – getting top marks at school, making it into a top university, securing a top job, and being paid a top income. Alternatively, for those who prefer short cuts, success is becoming a YouTube star and driving around in a black Lamborghini. But is that really what a successful life is?

Jesus has a very different idea of true success: 'I am the vine; you are the branches. Whoever abides in me and I in him, he it is that bears much fruit' (John 15:5). He was with his followers the night before he was to be killed and taken from them. These are some of his final instructions. He tells them, and us, how to make life count. According to Jesus, a successful life is a fruit-ful life. But what does that mean? And how do we get there?

Fruitful life

In this image Jesus uses, he is the vine and his people are the branches. If you're a vine branch, your purpose is clear – to bear fruit. A 'successful' branch is one with grapes on it. That's what the branch is for, and so it is with people. God's purpose for us is that we 'bear fruit', that we live fruitful lives – that is success.

In the Bible, fruit is often used as a picture of godly character and behaviour. In the Old Testament, the people of God are pictured as a vineyard; the good fruit they were supposed to produce was righteousness and justice, but, instead, they bore the bad fruit of drunken parties, materialism, injustice, corruption, and ignoring God (Isaiah 5).

A fruitful life is a life lived in a way that pleases God. God's design for us is to bear 'fruit in every good work' (Colossians 1:10). It's about the people we are, our char-acter and behaviour: doing good in loving and serving others and looking out towards others, rather than being curled in on ourselves.

The fruit image comes up in another passage that describes the 'fruit of the Spirit': 'love, joy, peace, patience, kindness, goodness, faithfulness, gentleness, self-control' (Galatians 5:22–23). These qualities are the good fruit that God wants in our lives.

The only person ever to live out this fruitful life 100%, 24/7, was Jesus Christ. Those who are his followers will be all too aware of how far they fall short of this, but they take heart from the command to bear 'fruit in keeping with repentance' (Matthew 3:8). A mark of the fruitful life is not perfection but being committed to continual repentance – turning from what is wrong as we become aware of it.

And as God's people live such fruitful lives, living out and sharing the gospel – the message about Jesus – so there is the fruit of others becoming joined to the vine themselves. The gospel is 'in the whole world . . . bearing fruit and growing' (Colossians 1:6).

Now, if success in God's eyes is a fruitful life, that's encouraging because it means that, to make your life count, you don't need to get to the top in your career (and, let's face it, most of us won't). It's not about that. It's about the person you are and the way you behave.

That's a very different value system; a different measure of success. It means your life can be a success even if you lose your job, if you're a stay-at-home parent, if you do a job that others look down on, or if you spend your life as a carer for a family member.

It's encouraging, but also challenging because it means that it's possible to be a great success in the world's eyes and your own, but to have wasted your life in God's eyes. An unfruitful life – nothing could be worse.

Wasted life

Jesus tells us what happens to branches that don't bear fruit:

> Every branch in me that does not bear fruit he [God the Father] takes away . . . If anyone does not abide in me, he is thrown away like a branch and withers; and the branches are gathered, thrown into the fire, and burned.
> (John 15:2, 6)

A fruitless life pictures an ungodly life. We've noted already some marks of such a life – drunkenness, materialism, corruption, and injustice. Also, in the passage about the fruit of the Spirit, that good fruit is contrasted with sexual immorality, impurity, enmity, jealousy, envy, 'and things like these' (Galatians 5:19–21) – bad works instead of good works.

In God's eyes, such a life is a wasted life. It doesn't matter if you got top marks and went to the best university, and reached the summit in your career and made shedloads of money – if you're fruitless, you're a failure and your life is wasted because the point of a vine branch is to bear fruit. That's what we're on the planet for.

Branches that don't do that wither (John 15:6). It's a picture of a dried-out life and character, of a person, although perhaps outwardly successful, who's shrivelled up – just a shell. The fate of such people is to be 'thrown into the fire, and burned' (15:6), which is a picture of final judgment. A fruitful life is not just a nice-to-have item; it's essential. In the end, it's fruit or fire.

So how do we get this fruitful life and become such fruitful branches? The answer is – through Jesus.

Get attached

You don't need to be a gardening expert to work out that there's only one way a vine branch produces grapes: it is by being attached to a vine. The vine is the source of life and fruitfulness.

So, what is the vine to which we need to be attached? Jesus says, 'I am the true vine . . . I am the vine; you are the branches' (John 15:1, 5). To live a fruitful life, we need to be united with him. In the Old Testament, the people of Israel were supposed to be the vine but they failed. They didn't produce the fruit God wanted. So, God sent Jesus, the Son of God, as the true vine, and we need to be in him to bear good fruit. The New Testament hardly ever uses the term 'Christian'. Instead, it talks about a person being 'in Christ' – united to him.

How do you become 'in Christ', a branch attached to Jesus, the true vine? Through faith; through putting your trust in Jesus and his death for you, not through good works. The purpose of a branch is to bear fruit, but you don't become a branch through bearing fruit: 'a person is not justified by works of the law but through faith in Jesus Christ' (Galatians 2:16).

A common misconception is that 'God accepts those who do good'; that if you do enough good, and it outweighs the bad, you'll be right with God. Even many a churchgoer operates with this wrong assumption. Jesus is saying, though, that the good life doesn't get you right with God. Instead, it's a fruit of being right with God through Jesus – the one who laid 'down his life for his friends' (John 15:13), dying so that we might be forgiven.

Once we are united with Jesus, the fruitful life flows from that. We are totally dependent on him. He says that 'apart from [him we] can do nothing' (15:5). We are as dependent on Christ for spiritual life and fruitfulness as a baby in the womb is dependent on its mother, getting all it needs through the umbilical cord. It's very humbling. However brilliant or determined you may be, apart from Christ, you're a withered stick.

Christmas trees

Does this mean that apart from Jesus it's impossible to bear good fruit? Apart from Jesus can someone not do any good?

In some sense they can: an atheist mum can still love her child; a Muslim worker can still be kind to his colleagues; a Hindu couple can still be faithful to each other. But if these acts are not the fruit of faith in Christ – a result of being united with his life and the outworking of a heart changed by the Spirit – they cannot ultimately please God: 'without faith it is impossible to please him' (Hebrews 11:6).

It's the difference between a vine and a Christmas tree. They may both look attractive – the vine with its bunches of grapes, the Christmas tree with its shiny baubles, lights, and tinsel. But one is alive; the other is dead. One is growing and producing fruit; the other will soon wither, drop its needles all over your living-room floor, and be thrown away and burned. That is why it's so vital that we become branches in the true vine. It's our only hope – to be in him and to remain, or abide, in him.

Abide in me

The point about abiding is repeated throughout the passage: 'Abide in me . . . whoever abides in me . . . if you abide in me' (John 15:4, 5, 7). Once in Jesus Christ, our responsibility is to remain in him. If we do, then we'll bear fruit: 'Whoever abides in me and I in him, he it is that bears much fruit' (15:5). If we don't, Jesus says, 'If anyone does not abide in me, he is thrown away like a branch and withers' (15:6). Those in Jesus need to remain in him. Everything hangs on this.

How do we do that? Jesus says, 'If you abide in me . . . my words abide in you' (15:7). Jesus' words are his teaching. Continuing in him means continuing in his teaching and seeking to obey him: 'If you keep my commandments, you will abide in my love . . . This is my commandment, that you love one another as I have loved you' (15:10, 12).

So, the Bible has a central place in the 'remain' life: reading it; living by it. The 'remain' life is a life committed to obeying Christ. But it's not an obedience that comes just from our own effort and willpower; it's an obedience empowered by Christ through the Spirit. Obedience is a fruit of being in him.

I'm surely not the only parent who has made the mistake of giving a child a gadget or toy as a present, only to discover, when he or she unwrapped it, these fateful words on the box: 'batteries not included'. The balloon of the child's initial delight deflates with disappointment, as your search through every drawer in the house yields nothing. The Christian life isn't like that – the batteries *are* included.

But the power supply doesn't just flow automatically. We need to ask God. The act of prayer is a recognition of our total dependence on him:

If you abide in me, and my words abide in you, ask whatever you wish, and it will be done for you. By this my Father is glorified, that you bear much fruit and so prove to be my disciples.
(15:7–8)

To be fruitful, we need to ask God; that is what the asking is about here. It's asking God to produce good fruit through us. The promise of 'whatever you wish', if you pray hard enough, does not mean that a shiny red Ferrari will be parked outside your house tomorrow morning.

Painful pruning

The fruitful life is also painful: 'I am the true vine, and my Father is the vine dresser. Every branch in me that does not bear fruit he takes away, and every branch that does bear fruit he prunes, that it may bear more fruit' (John 15:1–2). Pruning is cutting away bits of a plant or tree to make it more fruitful. If you're a branch, that's painful surgery.

Pruning is essential. To quote from no less an authority than the University of Missouri Department of Horticulture, 'Pruning is one of the most important and most neglected practices in home planting of grapes. Regular, purposeful pruning is essential for controlling the yield and quality of the fruit.'[3] Well, God the Father is an expert gardener, and he is committed to regular, purposeful pruning.

Jesus does not tell us in this passage what that involves but, elsewhere, the Bible describes how God uses hardships and difficulties to produce the 'fruit of righteousness' (Hebrews 12:11) in his people. He allows hard times, disappointments, setbacks, and sorrows to cut back unfruitful things in our lives and character, so that we bear even more fruit. It means that being fruitful is going to be painful.

Pure joy

Being fruitful is also joyful. 'These things I have spoken to you, that my joy may be in you, and that your joy may be full' (John 15:11). Religion, in the sense of a guilt-ridden, weary treadmill of duties, performed to try to gain acceptance by God, is not a joyful business. But being in Christ is.

There's the joy of living a fruitful life – the promise is of 'much fruit' (15:5, 8). There's also joy because at the heart of this fruitful life is relationship with Jesus, who loves his people: 'As the Father has loved me, so have I loved you. Abide in my love . . . love one another as I have loved you . . . You are my friends if you do what I command' (15:9, 12, 14). The branches are friends of Jesus, loved by him. That's very different from the distant, cold attitude to God that you find in Christ-less religion.

Jonathan Aitken, the former politician mentioned on page 7, describes how he used to relate to God before he came to Christ:

> The relationship I had with God was not unlike the one I had with the local bank manager in the country town where I grew up. I knew he existed, and that he was a person of some importance who was to be respected. I spoke to him politely, visited his premises intermittently, occasionally asked him for a small favour or overdraft to get myself out of difficulty, thanked him condescendingly for his assistance, kept up the appearance of being one of his reasonably reliable customers, and maintained superficial contact with him on the grounds that one of these days he might come in useful.[4]

This statement is in stark contrast to the relationship of love and friendship with Jesus Christ that Jonathan came to enjoy.

There's also the joy of knowing that a life lived for God ultimately brings glory to him: 'By this my Father is glorified, that you bear much fruit' (15:8). It's the joy of not making a name for yourself but a name for the one who really does deserve it; the joy of living for something – and someone – greater than yourself.

Right ambition

Is it wrong to be ambitious, and to want to be successful?

It depends. Ambitious for what? Successful in what? If my driving ambition is to make a name for myself, get as much money as possible, and live as comfortably as I can, I'm going to end up wasting my life.

A successful life is a fruitful life. Being in Jesus through faith, remaining in him, and bearing much fruit, in a life of growing godly character, good works, and service. The ambition God wants us to have is for a fruitful life, through knowing Jesus, that will bring joy to us, good to others, and glory to him. If that is our goal, we'll be on the right track – in this life and in the life to come.

I am
John 8:58

One day there'll be a headstone in a cemetery some-where. Engraved on it will be your name and two dates joined by a dash. That dash represents your life. If only that short dash were longer or, even better, if only the line kept going.

On the side of a building in London's Brick Lane is a sundial from 1743. It bears the motto from the Roman poet Horace: *umbra sumus*, Latin for 'we are a shadow'. Our lives are as brief as the shadow that moves across the sundial and then is gone. The Bible uses similar imagery:

> Man is like a breath;
>   his days are like a passing shadow.
> (Psalm 144:4)

When you're outside on a cold day, you see your breath and then it's gone. Life is like that.

Time flies, as we are constantly reminded by sundials on buildings, watches on our wrists, and clocks on our mobiles, computer screens, and walls. Time is passing – tick-tock – relentlessly, and we can't stop it.

We speak of saving time but we can't. We can only spend it. We can try to manage it better but we can't increase it. Money can't buy more hours and scientists can't invent more minutes. Each of us has only a finite amount of time. The sand is running through the hourglass and, all too soon, our time will be up. What then?

In all of us, there is a longing to escape the limitations of being finite, of having a beginning and an end. People who go to prison speak of 'doing time', but the reality is that we're all 'doing time'. Time is like a prison. It's as if we're born and live and die in a closed space, in a room with no way out. We wonder what is outside. We dream of the freedom of the big outdoors, the outside world. We don't just want tips on time-management – we want to break out. But that would have to be an outside job, and no-one has ever come from the outside. Or have they?

Jesus said, 'Before Abraham was, I am' (John 8:58). It's as if we're sitting in an enclosed space and, suddenly, a door opens, and in walks a man from outside time, claiming to be infinite, eternal, and that he can set us free.

In the course of this book, we've considered some remarkable 'I am' sayings of Jesus. This final one, though, is the most astonishing of all. No picture this time. Instead, just the simple statement 'I am'. This one is the foundation of all the others. It takes us to the very heart of who Jesus is and why he can meet our deepest needs.

To understand it, we're going to consider three sets of relationships: Jesus and Abraham; Jesus and the Father; and Jesus and us.

What Abraham saw

Abraham was the father of the Jewish nation. His story is told in the book of Genesis. He lived 1,800 years before Jesus. When speaking with some Jews, Jesus said, 'Your father Abraham rejoiced that he would see my day. He saw it and was glad' (John 8:56). There are three things Jesus is claiming there.

First, that he, Jesus, is the Messiah. God had promised Abraham that blessing would come to the whole world through one of his descendants. That was 'the day' Abraham looked forward to – the day this person would come. Jesus referred to it as 'my day'. Jesus saw himself as the fulfilment of that ancient promise about the arrival of the rescuer King.

Second, Jesus was saying that, for Abraham, death was not the end. Jesus said, 'Abraham rejoiced that he would see my day. He saw it and was glad' (8:56). Abraham died almost two millennia before Jesus and yet he saw the day when Jesus the Messiah would come. He saw it for himself, with his own eyes. How is that possible? It's possible only if Abraham lived on after death, in heaven.

In the Old Testament, long after Abraham had died, God said, 'I am the God of Abraham, and the God of Isaac, and the God of Jacob.' Jesus quoted this and then commented, 'He is not God of the dead, but of the living' (Matthew 22:32). For those, like Abraham, who know God, life goes on with God after death.

Whenever another year comes to an end, the media look back on the lives of the rich and famous who have died over the past twelve months. But for such celebrities, only one thing matters now – did they know God? Are they living on with God, like Abraham?

Third, Jesus was claiming to have been with Abraham in heaven. Jesus said, 'Your father Abraham rejoiced that he would see my day. He saw it and was glad' (John 8:56). How did Jesus know that? How did he know that Abraham was glad to see for himself the day when the Messiah would be sent into the world?

The only way he could have known that was if he, Jesus, had been with Abraham when it happened. He witnessed Abraham's joy the day that he, the Son of God, left heaven to come to earth and be born as a man.

Those listening to Jesus clearly understood that this was what he was claiming: 'So the Jews said to him, "You are not yet fifty years old, and have you seen Abraham?"' (8:57). Yes, he had. He was with Abraham in heaven. It was from heaven that Jesus came. He said that explicitly on numerous occasions:

I am the living bread that came down from heaven . . . You are from below; I am from above. You are of this world; I am not of this world . . . I came from God and I am here.
(John 6:51; 8:23, 42)

Race against time

Breaking 2 is a documentary about the attempt, on 6 May 2017, to break the two-hour marathon barrier. Three runners took up the challenge. One of them, the Kenyan runner Eliud Kipchoge, says at the beginning of the film: 'I really want to be the first one under two hours. I want to tell the world that no human is limited.' Although a two-hour marathon is absurdly fast (and, in 2019, Kipchoge did manage it), it doesn't actually demonstrate that 'no human is limited'. We are limited. We are finite. And Kipchoge, just like the rest of us, is in a race against time, which, in the end, he's going to lose. He'll get old, he'll slow down, and one day he'll die.

We are limited. That's precisely part of the problem. But in Jesus, we come into contact with someone who is not; someone who has come from outside time, down from heaven. In Jesus, we come face to face with the infinite. And that becomes even clearer when he says, 'Before Abraham was, I am' (John 8:58). Not only was Jesus with Abraham in heaven but he also says he was alive before Abraham. Abraham lived eighteen centuries before Jesus, but Jesus asserts, very matter-of-factly, that he was around before him.

Not 'I was' but 'I am'. In the Bible, there is just one being in the universe who is eternally present, everlasting, and immortal – God himself: 'from everlasting to everlasting you are God' (Psalm 90:2); Abraham 'called . . . on the name of the LORD, the Everlasting God' (Genesis 21:33); and God 'alone has immortality'

(1 Timothy 6:16). Jesus' statement is nothing less than a claim to be divine.

Rolex and Omega vie with each other for the top spot as the premier luxury watch brand. In the James Bond film *Casino Royale*, the character Vesper Lynd looks at 007's watch and says, 'Rolex?'

'Omega,' he replies.

The rivalry has been going on for years. Mercedes Gleitze became the first British woman to swim the English Channel in 1927. She did it wearing a water-proof Rolex Oyster round her neck – a great marketing coup for Rolex. An Omega watch, however, became the first one to make it to the Moon, on Buzz Aldrin's wrist.

To own a Rolex or an Omega watch is a statement of how rich and powerful you are. But, ironically, it's also a constant reminder of how powerless you are. Your time is ticking away, just like everyone else's. In Jesus, though, we encounter the infinite. The eternal God in human form. But what exactly does that mean? How does Jesus relate to God the Father?

Father and Son

Jesus is distinct from the Father. Jesus highlighted this: 'I honour my Father . . . It is my Father who glorifies me, of whom you say, "He is our God"' (John 8:49, 54). The majestic opening of John's Gospel declares, 'In the beginning was the Word, and the Word was with God . . . And the Word became flesh and dwelt among us, and we have seen his glory, glory as of the only Son from the Father' (John 1:1, 14). Jesus is the eternal Word, the Son, who was with God the Father from all eternity. Jesus prays to God the Father saying, 'And now, Father, glorify me in your own presence with the glory that I had with you before the world existed' (John 17:5).

So, Jesus as the Son is distinct from the Father. He is also one with the Father. He said, 'I and the Father are one . . . Whoever has seen me has seen the Father . . . I am in the Father and the Father is in me' (John 10:30; 14:9, 10). The Jews sought to kill him because he was 'making himself equal with God' (John 5:18).

His oneness with God the Father is evident in Jesus' saying, 'Before Abraham was, I am' (John 8:58). 'I am' is actually the name by which the Creator God revealed himself in the Old Testament. The book of Exodus records an encounter Moses had with God, in which Moses asked him what his name is. God replied, 'I AM WHO I AM . . . Say this to the people of Israel, "I AM has sent me to you"' (Exodus 3:14).

Stone him

The significance of what Jesus was saying was not lost on the Jews of his day: 'So they picked up stones to throw at him' (John 8:59). They were in no doubt that he was claiming to be God; that is why they were going to stone him to death – for blasphemy.

We find the same reaction after Jesus said, 'I and the Father are one.' The Jews responded, 'It is not for a good work that we are going to stone you but for blasphemy, because you, being a man, make yourself God' (John 10:33). Notice that Jesus didn't respond by saying, 'Look guys, you've misunderstood. You've got the wrong end of the stick. I wasn't claiming anything of the sort.' Sometimes, people say that Jesus never claimed to be God. Well, people at the time clearly believed that he did.

The Jews asked him, 'Who do you make yourself out to be?' (John 8:53). It's a good question, and this is his answer: he's not just a good teacher, not just a wise prophet, and not just a great leader; he is none other than the eternal God become man, distinct from the Father and yet one with the Father.

A claim of that magnitude raises the stakes for all of us. What do we make of him? How will we respond to him? What about Jesus and us?

Many of those listening to him rejected his claim, as many still do today. They accused him of being demon-possessed (8:48, 52). They picked up stones to stone him to death (8:59). They wanted to silence him; get rid of him; and put him in his place – with nails if necessary.

They had their own agenda and Jesus did not feature on it. They had their own world view and religious system and Jesus did not fit into it. They had their own high opinion of themselves and their own goodness and Jesus did not agree with it.

But what matters more than their verdict on Jesus is his verdict on them – and on us. He said that their claim to know God was false: 'you have not known him' (8:55). He called them liars for claiming to know God, when in fact they didn't. Jesus didn't pull his punches. According to him, if anyone rejects his claims and says they know God, they're lying or they're deceived. It is only through Jesus that anyone can know God.

Trapped in time

We began by thinking about a sundial with the inscription *umbra sumus*. The building it is on has had quite a varied history. It was built by French Protestants as a chapel in 1743. In 1891, it became a Jewish synagogue. Then, in 1976, it was turned into a mosque, serving the local Bangladeshi community. It has housed Christians, Jews, and Muslims.

But Jesus says that being religious is not sufficient. To know God, we have to do what Jesus says: 'if anyone keeps my word, he [or she] will never see death' (John 8:51). If we refuse to follow and obey him, we don't know God. And we remain trapped in time, with no answer to death, after which we will meet God in his role as judge (8:50). If we reject Jesus, we miss out on everything he offers – both this side of the grave and beyond. We miss out on everything we've explored in the 'I am' sayings throughout this book.

If we reject him, in so doing we have to trample over a mountain of evidence that he provided to support his claims. There's the evidence of his character: 'Which one of you convicts me of sin?' he said to his opponents (8:46). No-one could. Even his enemies had nothing to pin on him. He lived the perfect life.

There's the evidence of the Old Testament prophecies, fulfilled in the details of his birth, life, death, and resurrection. There's the evidence of his miracles. Jesus said, 'Even though you do not believe me, believe the works, that you may know and understand that the Father is in me and I am in the Father' (John 10:38).

The incident we've looked at in this chapter ends with the words: 'but Jesus hid himself and went out of the temple' (John 8:59). That's the worst thing that can happen to anyone – for Jesus to leave you; withdraw from you; hide from you. But if we say to Jesus that we don't want him in our lives, in the end he will grant that request. We will be shut out from his presence, away from him and his goodness – for ever.

Sharing his life

That is not, however, what Jesus wants. The reason he stepped into time, the reason he came from heaven, was not to gloat. It wasn't to mock us. It wasn't to say, 'I'm infinite but you're not. You're finite. Ha, ha.' It was to share his eternal life with us.

He stepped into time – and allowed himself, the eternal one, to be constrained by time and then by death – in order to set us free: free from the prison of time counting down; free from the curse of being finite; free from death.

He promised that if 'anyone keeps [his] word, he [or she] will never see death' (8:51). On your headstone will be two dates, with a dash in between. But then, after the second date, there will be a line continuing and going on for ever, to infinity, with Jesus.

The watches of Patek Philippe, the Swiss luxury watch manufacturer, have adorned many famous wrists – those of Leo Tolstoy, Queen Victoria, and Richard Wagner, to name a few. The company's publicity now typically shows a father with his son. The tagline is 'You never actually own a Patek Philippe. You merely look after it for the next generation.' It reassures the consumer that Patek Philippe watches are so well made they'll stand the test of time. But it's also unsettling to think that your watch might outlive you, that it might survive you and be passed on to the next generation when your time is up.

Life is so short. The clock is ticking. What can your world view offer you when the final grain of sand runs through the hourglass of your life? In our race against time, we need more than time-management gurus. We need Jesus.

We need the one who says, 'Before Abraham was, I am.' The one who, like the groom at a wedding, vows, 'All that I have I share with you.' In Jesus, the infinite, eternal Creator has come to share his eternal life with us, finite creatures, whose lives are just a shadow and a mere breath.

'If anyone keeps my word, he will never see death.'

EPILOGUE

Pills and puff!

When the landlord kicked down the door of the flat in New Cross, London, he found two babies lying in a corner. They were crying, alone, abandoned. Twin boys. One of them, Jason (Jay), was placed with a foster family, the Marriners, in Brixton, with ten other kids, each with his or her own tragic backstory. Winston, one of the others, had a scar on his face from when his parents had poured hot porridge over him. In different ways, all of them were scarred.

At primary school, Jay would just mess about and skive off. Secondary school was no better. He had zero interest in education. He was suspended three times and finally expelled for burning down the science lab. He left school with one GCSE qualification – a D in pottery.

In his teens, Jay got into clubbing, drinking, and taking drugs. The rave scene hit London in the late 1980s, and he and his mates would end up going several times a week to dance through the night in fields packed with tens of thousands of other young people.

At one such event, at about 4 a.m., a man walked past him, with a bucket in each hand, calling out, 'Pills and puff! Pills and puff!' He was selling ecstasy and cannabis.

Jay realized that money was to be made, and so he began a career in the drugs trade.

One night, a few years later, at the Ministry of Sound club, he was caught red-handed, with one pocket full of ecstasy pills and the other stuffed with bank notes. The bouncers marched him out; he was arrested, tried, convicted, and sentenced to four years in Belmarsh Prison.

Six months into his sentence, he sat on his bed and vented his anger: 'God, if you are there, you owe me. I've never killed anyone; never robbed anyone. I give up my seat on the bus for old ladies. I wear my poppy at Remembrance. I'm just a good, honest drug dealer.'

When he'd done his time and was released, he went straight back into the drugs business. He'd learned nothing at all. In fact, he moved up a gear and joined forces with some 'proper villains', as he called them, importing cocaine into the country. It involved night-time pick-ups from boats on remote beaches and large sums of money in plastic carrier bags. But he ended up losing it all.

Surprise visits

Then one day, out of the blue, his girlfriend started going to a local church and became a Christian. When she told him, Jay tore their kitchen apart in a rage, ripping cabinets off the walls and smashing the door in pieces. He wanted nothing to do with God.

But a week later, the pastor of her church turned up on their doorstep. He came into the living room, turned off the TV, sat down, and began to tell Jay about Jesus. Jay's response was to the point: 'Either you leave through the window or I'll post you through the letter box.'

Two weeks later, he opened the door and it was the pastor again. This time he had with him a group of Christians, who scurried past into the living room, got their Bibles out, and proceeded to have a Bible study. Some of the verses Jay heard them discussing said that 'all have sinned and fall short of the glory of God' (Romans 3:23) and that 'the wages of sin is death, but the free gift of God is eternal life in Christ Jesus our Lord' (Romans 6:23).

The next day Jay rang one of his mates in a daze. 'Nick,' he said, 'it was like the Bible was alive. It spoke about my life. It made sense.' He got on his knees and prayed. He even wrote on the wall a list of behaviours he was going to stop.

But months passed and nothing changed. One morning, he returned home, having been out all night yet again with his mates, and he could see the disappointment on his girlfriend's face. 'What do you expect of me?' he protested. 'I've never looked into the eyes of my dad. I've grown up in care. Jason Marriner is who I am. I can't do this.'

At that moment, it was as if he heard God saying in his heart, 'That's right, you can't do it. Jesus has already done it.' And the penny dropped – he realized that the good news is that it's not about what we do, but about what Jesus has done for us. He died for us and was raised to life, and is calling us to trust in him.

So, Jay began a new life of following Jesus. He met up with a Christian guy called John, who read the Bible with him and explained what it meant. They went through Mark's Gospel together. 'The more I read it,' said Jay, 'the more I met with Jesus. It wasn't easy. There was a lot to change.'

Jay resolved early on that, just as he'd been hardcore on the streets, he was going to be hardcore for Jesus. And he was, and still is. He and his girlfriend got married, and decided to go back to Brixton where he had grown up – not to sell drugs but to start a church; a church for a community littered with Jay Marriners.

'The gospel changed my life. I want Jesus to be known. The way I was broken and broke lives – only Jesus could fix the mess.'

Another planet

Mark Harding was born just half an hour south of where Jay was found abandoned as a baby – but into a very different world. He came from a loving family in Beckenham and attended an independent school in Sevenoaks. He gained a degree in Modern Languages and Law at Cambridge and went on to law school. He became a partner at Clifford Chance, heading up its International Financial Markets Group. A few moves later, he became the Group General Counsel at Barclays, responsible for all the legal and compliance work throughout the bank worldwide, leading a staff of more than a thousand. At the time, he was arguably the most high-profile and influential General Counsel in the FTSE 100. Mark loves opera and the arts, plays golf, is mad keen on cricket, and is a member of the Marylebone Cricket Club (MCC).

On so many levels, the lives of Jay and Mark could not have been more different. It's as if they came from different planets. But they now have one thing in common: they've both been transformed by the person who is the subject of this book. Mark was not from a Christian home. His family would pitch up at church at Christmas and Easter but nothing more. At school, however, he and some others started asking the same questions about life, and were introduced to the Jesus of the Bible by a Christian teacher.

Although on the surface Mark and Jay as teenagers would have seemed poles apart, Mark became aware that he had the same fundamental problem: 'Every one of us naturally puts ourselves at the centre of our lives, and not the God who made us,' and that God will call us to account.

Having examined the evidence, he was persuaded of the same solution – that Jesus really did die for us and was raised to life: 'It's only in Jesus that you will find real truth, real hope for the future, real peace with God. The name of Jesus is powerful.'

Still in the business

So, at the age of 17, Mark started following Jesus. Now, a lifetime later, he and those school friends are still on that same path: 'I've walked with Jesus, and with them, all through my life.' And he is as hardcore for Jesus as Jay is; living all out for him.

The London City Mission was founded to get the good news of Jesus out to the most marginalized in the capital. Mark has been a trustee for twenty-nine years and the chairman for twelve. He's passionate about knowing Jesus and making him known: 'Jesus Christ is still in the business today of rescuing people from their sins and giving them eternal life.'

Jesus is still in the business because he was raised to life and is alive today. The one who said 'I am the bread of life' some two thousand years ago is still the bread of life today. He invites us to come to him, to feed on him, to trust personally in him, and to begin a new life with him, as Mark has, as Jay has, and as have countless millions of others, from every country and culture.

I see this even at our own small floating church which started in 2004, where there are people from all around the world, who have grown up in such diverse cultures but who have been drawn together by the one thing they have in common – a personal experience of the transforming power of Jesus Christ. They are from Singapore, Hong Kong, Switzerland, Japan, Sweden, South Africa, China, Uzbekistan, Australia, New Zealand, Vietnam, Russia, Peru, Finland, France, Brazil, Canada, India, Italy, Sri Lanka, South Korea, Nigeria, Malaysia, Germany, Zimbabwe, Indonesia, and Hungary – plus a few from the British Isles as well! The list could go on. All of us at the church, like so many little planets, have come into orbit around the same sun. Like so many moths, we've have come out of the darkness to gather round the same light.

Taste and see

But don't just take our word for it. Why not taste and see for yourself? All of us at church have, at some point, begun relating to God through Jesus. That's how the Christian life begins. You could do the same.

There's no 'abracadabra' formula of magical words, but the kind of thing to say to God could be summed up simply in three of the first terms you teach a child: 'sorry', 'thank you', 'please'. Here is an example of what you could say to God:

> Lord God, I recognize that I've gone my own way in life and deserve your judgment. I'm *sorry* for doing that and I turn from it. *Thank you* for sending Jesus into the world to die as my rescuer and to be raised to life as my ruler. I believe the 'I am' claims he made are true. *Please* accept me now through him. Forgive me, fill me with your Holy Spirit, and strengthen me to follow Jesus for the rest of my life.

On taking that step, a new life begins. Jesus describes it as being 'born again' (John 3:3). You now have a new birthday, which is something to celebrate – so don't keep it to yourself. Do tell others. It's a great day!

The moment you put your trust in Jesus, God becomes your loving heavenly Father. He forgives you and assures you that you have crossed from death to life and now have nothing to fear from the coming judgment (John 5:24). Instead, you can look forward to eternal life with him and his people in a renewed world.

But the present isn't just about waiting for that future. Life now has a new direction and purpose. It's about getting to know God better and living for him each day. He has given us all the resources we need to do that. Here are four key ones.

First, the Spirit: on receiving Jesus, God comes into your life by his Holy Spirit, to be with you, to help you, and to change you.

Second, the Bible:[1] the Bible is God's word and is the main way God communicates with us, so it's important to read it each day.[2] Through it, we learn more about him and how he wants us to live.

Third, prayer: prayer is simply talking to God. We can talk to him about anything and everything, but some people find the acronym **STOP** a helpful structure: **S**orry (we say sorry to God for things we've done wrong, and we turn from them); **T**hank you (we thank God for all his good gifts); **O**thers (we pray for the needs of others we know); **P**lease (we pray for things that we need for ourselves).

Fourth, church: through trusting in Jesus, you become part of God's family, which means you have new brothers and sisters in Christ. As family, we are to encourage, support, and serve one another. That's why joining a local church family of people – who believe Jesus' claims and are following him – is so vital. We're not supposed to live the Christian life alone. If you would like help in finding a good local church, do get in touch.[3]

A closer look

But it may be that starting to follow Jesus is not where you're at; you're not ready to take that step yet, but would like to find out more. How could you do that?

Well, you could read through John's Gospel, in which these 'I am' sayings are recorded – either on your own or with a Christian, if you know one. Why not ask your Christian friend to meet up with you to go through it?[4]

You could check out an introductory course, such as Christianity Explored or Alpha, which many churches run. The course websites will give you details of one near you and will also have other resources.[5] In fact, going along to church services is a good way to explore further. Church is just as much for the seeker as for the believer.

You could read the stories of how others have come to follow Jesus in a book such as *City Lives*.[6] If you have questions but don't know other Christians you could ask, feel free to contact me.

In the end, Christianity is Christ. It's all about Jesus. He is the bread of life; the light of the world; the door; the good shepherd; the resurrection and the life; the way, the truth, and the life; the vine; the I am.

If these claims are true, nothing could be more important. If they're not, it's the biggest con in history. But what they can't be – and what Jesus can't be – is just vaguely interesting. Far too much is at stake for that.

NOTES

Introduction

1 Story adapted from Tom Holland, *Rubicon: The triumph and tragedy of the Roman Republic* (London: Little, Brown, 2003), p. 1; Aulus Gellius, *Noctes Atticae* (Loeb Edition), bk 1:xix, quoted in 'King Tarquin and the Sibylline Books', 10 July 2015, <https://stalkingtime.wordpress.com/2015/07/10/king-tarquin-and-the-sibylline-books>, accessed 13 October 2020.

I am THE BREAD

1 Leo Nikolayevich Tolstoy, *A Confession* (Grand Rapids, Mich.: Christian Classics Ethereal Library, n.d.), p. 16; <www.ccel.org/ccel/t/tolstoy/confession/cache/confession.pdf>, accessed 10 September 2020.

2 Tolstoy, *A Confession*, p. 13.

3 Jonathan Aitken, *Pride and Perjury: An autobiography* (London: HarperCollins, 2000), p. 9.

4 Tolstoy, *A Confession*, p. 40.

I am THE LIGHT

1 Quoted in Marcus Nodder, *City Lives: True stories of changed lives from the workplace* (Leyland: 10Publishing, 2018), p. 158.

2 Quoted in Nodder, *City Lives*, p. 158.

3 From Louis Zamperini and David Rensin,
   *Devil at My Heels: A heroic Olympian's astonishing
   story of survival as a Japanese POW in World War II*
   (New York: HarperCollins, 2011), quoted in
   'Broken by grace', 17 August 2016, <https://
   northstar.church/broken-by-grace>, accessed
   12 September 2020.

I am THE DOOR

1 Will Hayward, 'How to survive your first 24 hours in
   prison', 13 January 2018, <www.walesonline.co.uk/
   news/wales-news/how-survive-your-first-24-14149578>,
   accessed 10 September 2020.
2 Timothy Keller, *The Reason for God: Belief in an
   age of skepticism* (New York: Dutton, 2008), p. 46.
3 Joni Eareckson Tada, 'Reflections on the 50th
   anniversary of my diving accident', 30 July 2017,
   <www.thegospelcoalition.org/article/reflections-
   on-50th-anniversary-of-my-diving-accident>,
   accessed 10 September 2020.

I am THE GOOD SHEPHERD

1 See <https://edition.cnn.com/2018/05/30/us/jesse-
   duplantis-plane-falcon-7x-prosperity-gospel-trnd/
   index.html>, accessed 10 September 2020.

I am THE RESURRECTION

1 *The Standard Edition of the Complete Psychological
   Works of Sigmund Freud* (London: The Hogarth
   Press, 1957), p. 289.

2 From Woody Allen, *Without Feathers* (New York: Grand Central Publishing, 1976), quoted in Miles Kington, 'Did I say that? You will, Spike, you will', 20 March 2002, <www.independent.co.uk/voices/columnists/miles-kington/did-i-say-that-you-will-spike-you-will-9167189.html>, accessed 10 September 2020.

3 Jim Denney, 'Can writing make you immortal?', 22 October 2012, <https://unearthlyfiction.wordpress.com/2012/10/22/can-writing-make-you-immortal>, accessed 10 September 2020. Denney is quoting Michael P. Kube-McDowell, who posted his comment on an Internet forum on 31 May 1991.

4 Quoted in Marcus Nodder, *City Lives: True stories of changed lives from the workplace* (Leyland: 10Publishing, 2018), p. 80.

5 Quoted in Nodder, *City Lives*, pp. 84–85.

6 Taken from the Committal in the service for the Burial of the Dead in *An English Prayer Book*, <http://churchsociety.org/docs/english_prayer_book/19_EPB_burial.pdf>, p. 6, accessed 10 September 2020.

I am THE WAY

1 Timothy Keller, *The Reason for God: Belief in an age of skepticism* (New York: Dutton, 2008), p. 3.

2 G. K. Chesterton, 'The House of Christmas', <http://www.gkc.org.uk/gkc/books/house.html>, accessed 10 September 2020.

3 C. S. Lewis, *Mere Christianity* (Collins Fount Paperbacks, 1990), pp. 118–119.

4 See <https://www.youtube.com/watch?v= 0kPINNhHGNw>, accessed 12 September 2020.

5 Lewis, *Mere Christianity*, p. 52.

I am THE VINE

1 Quoted in Emily Arata, 'Man tells heartbreaking story of how he realized he wasted his life', *Elite Daily*, 7 November 2014, <www.elitedaily.com/news/world/ man-writes-about-wasting-life/841316>, accessed 11 September 2020.

2 Anna Vital, 'Lost in Life? People who took an indirect path to success', <https://www.lifehack.org/338771/ why-its-never-too-late-to-do-something-great>, accessed 2 September 2020.

3 Michele R. Warmund, 'Home fruit production: Grape training systems', University of Missouri Extension, revised November 2014, <https://extension2.missouri. edu/g6090>, accessed 11 September 2020.

4 Quoted in Marcus Nodder, *City Lives: True stories of changed lives from the workplace* (Leyland: 10Publishing, 2018), pp. 132–133.

Epilogue

1 A good modern translation in English is the NIV (New International Version) or ESV (English Standard Version). You can access them online for free at <www.biblegateway.com>, but it's worth buying your own copy as well.

2 The Good Book Company produces Bible-reading notes for every age group, to help you with daily Bible reading: <www.thegoodbook.co.uk>.

3 You can contact me at <mnodder@gmail.com>.

4 Many people have found The Word One To One notes a great way to do that: <www.theword121.com>.

5 At <www.christianityexplored.org>, for example, there is a section on answers to tough questions.

6 Marcus Nodder, *City Lives: True stories of changed lives from the workplace* (Leyland: 10Publishing, 2018).

ACKNOWLEDGMENTS

I am so grateful to my parents for introducing me to the person who is the subject of this book; to my wife Lina and four children for their love; to the St Peter's Barge church family for the past sixteen years; to the staff team for the privilege of serving together; to the Friday morning Partnership guys for their friendship and support; to Eleanor Trotter and Louise Clairmonte for their editorial wisdom; and, last but not least, to Sally our beagle – for what exactly, I'm not sure, but I didn't want to leave her out!